KU-771-331

Robert W. Gill

BASIC RENDERING

Effective Drawing for Designers, Artists and Illustrators

with 255 illustrations

 Thames and Hudson

Any copy of this book issued by the publisher as a paperback
is sold subject to the condition that it shall not
by way of trade or otherwise be lent, resold, hired out or
otherwise circulated without the publisher's prior consent
in any form of binding or cover other than that in which
it is published and without a similar condition including
these words being imposed on a subsequent purchaser.

© 1991 Thames and Hudson Ltd, London

All Rights Reserved. No part of this publication
may be reproduced or transmitted in any form or by any means,
electronic or mechanical, including photocopy, recording or
any other information storage and retrieval system, without
prior permission in writing from the publisher.

Printed and bound in Yugoslavia

Contents

2 Giuseppe Galli Bibiena, *Jesuit Drama in Setting*, 1740. This engraving shows that rendering is the means by which the illusion of realism is produced in a line drawing.

Preface

Rendering is one of the most exciting and challenging aspects of producing pictures in any area of the graphic arts. Like every other aspect of the creative arts, rendering has principles that are based on truths evolved over a number of centuries. These principles are used to introduce the illusion of realism into two-dimensional representations of three-dimensional objects and views. In this context the term 'realism' means photographic realism, which is accepted in our society as the graphic truth.

Though rendering is a broad and complex subject it can be made much simpler if the basic principles are understood from the very beginning. The ability to understand and use these basic principles forms the foundation of visual literacy, which is essential to anyone wishing to practise in any area of art, design or graphics, and is attained by first learn-

8-95

Books are to be returned on or before
the last date below.

PONTYPRIDD TECHNICAL COLLEGE LIBRARY

12 DEC 1996

16 JAN 1997

2 7 FEB 1997

- 2 DEC 1997

5   1998

24 NOV 2003

0 7 DEC 2004

The Glamorgan Centre for
Art & Design Technology

021511

1 William Hogarth, frontispiece to *Kirby's Perspective*, Joshua Kirby's edition of *Dr Brook Taylor's Method of Perspective*, 1754. 'Whosoever makes a design without the knowledge of perspective, will be liable to such absurdities as are shown in this frontispiece.'

ing to see and understanding what is seen. In this context, I believe that seeing is a learned skill and to learn to see one must first learn how to look and what to look for. Objects are seen as complex images to which perspective, light and shade, shadows, values, contrasts, atmospheric effects, textures and colours all contribute. Consequently a great deal must be known about these elements and the principles of their graphic interpretation before what is seen can be understood and used for competent pictorial representations. Rendering, therefore, can be described as the process of interpreting graphically what is seen and what is known.

It is a fundamental truth that competent renderings in all areas of art and graphics must be based on accurate drawings, so the renderer must be thoroughly conversant with the principles of perspective projection, shadow projection and so on. In my opinion, the caption to the frontispiece to

3 Realism is the most striking aspect of this masterpiece of modern rendering by Paul Stevenson Oles, depicting the west front of Washington Cathedral.

4 Otto Wagner's perspective of the Post Office Savings Bank, Vienna, is both precise and decorative.

Kirby's Perspective, engraved by William Hogarth, makes the point best of all: 'Whosoever makes a design without the knowledge of perspective, will be liable to such absurdities as are shown in this frontispiece.'

I have dealt in detail with perspective in two previous books, *Basic Perspective* and *Creative Perspective* and do not intend to repeat the information here. Because of the importance of perspective drawing as a basis for rendering these two books are recommended. Unlike another of my books, *Rendering with Pen and Ink*, which dealt solely with the practicalities of rendering in that one medium, this book deals with the basic principles of rendering in simple terms, so that the student can understand not only what is seen under a specific set of conditions, but why it is seen in that particular way, and how this understanding can be put into practice in an enormous variety of artistic media. Simple objects, such as cubes, rectangular prisms, cylinders, cones and spheres have been used, and ordinary, uncomplicated conditions are described. By studying these simple objects and conditions, it is possible to establish a basic understanding which can be developed and expanded for more complex shapes and conditions.

Rendering is the means used to turn a simple line drawing into a pictorial representation consistent with actuality, that is, a two-dimensional representation of a three-dimensional object or view. Provided that the rendering offers an accu-

5 In this 1902 perspective drawing by Charles Rennie Mackintosh, the bare verticality of the building is countered by the flowing lines of the trees and sky.

rate image it can be of inestimable value as a communication between a designer and his client, and/or the public. A rendered drawing shows the observer a pictorial representation of an object or view as it would actually appear, even before the object is made or built, or the view re-landscaped, etc. Therefore the designer, whether in the fields of architecture, industrial design, interior design, landscape design or illustration, must be able to draw the object in perspective, complete with accurate light and shade and shadow projections, and be able to render the drawing using valid principles so that the result is an honest statement of fact. In other words, it is essential that a rendering purporting to represent the result of the specific design process conveys the true intent of that design.

Renderings are also an essential part of the design thinking process. Because design is essentially an intellectual process which relies on graphics as its language of communication, a designer must rely on graphics to give his ideas reality so that he can confirm every step in the design thinking process. This he can do with confidence only if he knows that his graphic images portray the truth, i.e. they are accurate and are based on visual facts. It is interesting to note that all of the world's leading designers, particularly in architecture, are or were highly competent delineators, for example Charles Rennie Mackintosh (5), Le Corbusier and Frank Lloyd Wright, as well as many others.

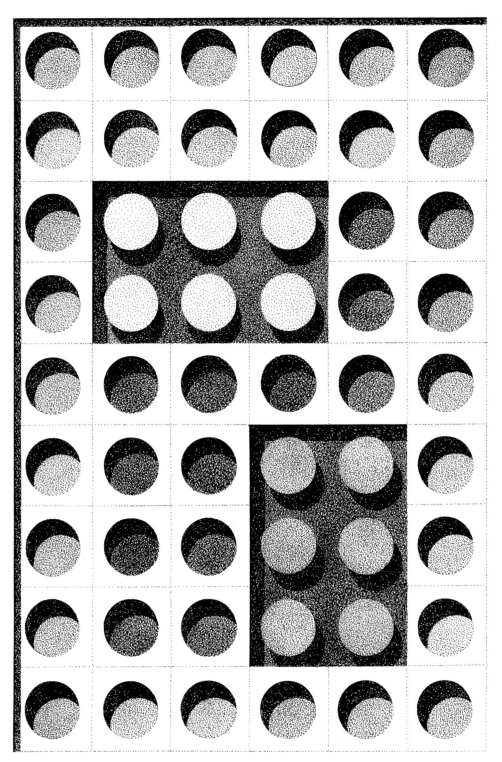

6 A rendered drawing is a two-dimensional representation which conveys information to an observer in a form which he or she understands because it is based on optical reality.

7 With the simplest of fluid outlines, Paul Klee created this hugely expressive self-portrait of 1919.

To portray the true intent of a design, a rendering must have as its principal objectives accuracy and honesty, i.e. integrity. It can and should have other qualities as well, but its first duty is to portray the design truthfully.

The purposes of rendering outside design might at first appear to be less demanding. However, it should be obvious that the artist must have the knowledge and skills necessary to communicate space, shape, form, light and shade, atmospheric effect, contrast, texture and colour, no matter what type of expression he chooses. The artist needs to understand the basic principles because it is only through the ability to understand and use these valid principles that he can produce a rendering that clearly communicates his intentions.

To sum up, a rendered drawing is a two-dimensional representation which conveys information to an observer in a form which can be understood, because it is based on principles that conform with what is seen. It reproduces the illusion of the conditions in a form that the eye recognizes as consistent with those seen when looking at an actual view or object. Therefore, the most convincing renderings are those which most accurately represent the conditions that exist in reality. Only a complete understanding of the basic principles and the acquisition of the essential skills to use, develop and expand them to individual requirements will result in competent renderings in art, design and graphics.

To learn to draw it is first
necessary to learn to see.

To learn to see it is first
necessary to learn to look.

To learn to look it is first
necessary to learn what to
look for.

To understand what is seen
it is necessary to learn the
basic principles involved in
seeing.

Drawing is a simple process
of interpreting graphically
what is seen and what is
known.

Knowledge and learned skills
are responsible for good
drawings, PRACTICE IS
RESPONSIBLE FOR BETTER ONES.

8 The importance of learning to see.

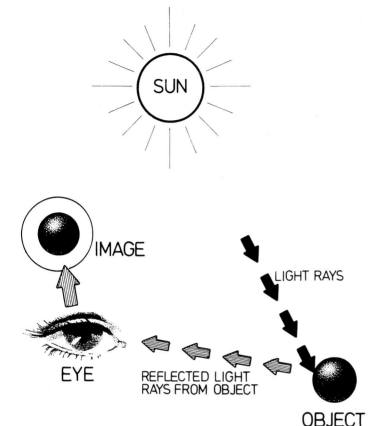

The seeing process

In order to learn to draw or paint, the student must first be taught to see as a means of gathering essential information. Normal human beings are born with the physical equipment for seeing, but most never develop this faculty beyond the minimum level required by the average person for general use, that is, for navigation, recognition, reading, etc. Greater efficiency in seeing as a means of gathering information is, in my opinion, a learned skill, like the skills of speaking, reading, writing, or riding a bicycle. Because of this, the process of learning to draw must start with learning to see and then follow a logical development of knowledge and skill.

Seeing is the basis of valid drawing skills, so it is necessary to understand the seeing process in its most elementary form. Because the human eye is a light-sensing organ, light must be present for it to be able to see.

For the eye to become activated, i.e. to see, light must strike an object and be reflected in the direction of the eye where an image of the object is recorded on the retina (**9**). Naturally, if no light strikes the object no light can be reflected from it, which means that the eye cannot see it.

10 Gustave Doré, *Opium Smoking: The Lascar's Room in 'Edwin Drood'*, engraving, 1872. Doré was a master of the manipulation of light to build effects and moods in his drawings.

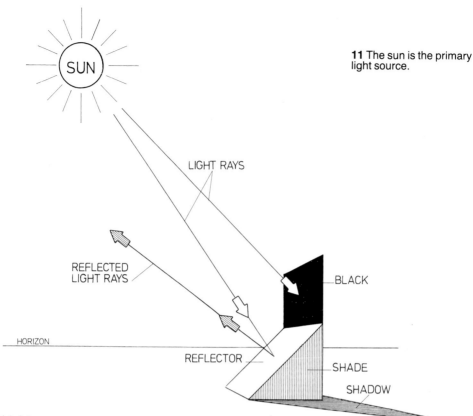

11 The sun is the primary light source.

Light

An understanding of the following information is essential to correct interpretation and portrayal of the effects of light in two-dimensional representations of three-dimensional objects or views.

1 Light is the basis of all seeing.
2 The sun is considered to be the primary light source for this planet.
3 Light is said to travel from its source in straight lines known as light rays.
4 Light rays cannot change direction unless they strike a reflector of some kind.
5 Light rays cannot penetrate solid, opaque matter and this results in shade and shadow.
6 All materials are capable of reflecting light rays to some degree. Any given material of a light value is capable of reflecting more light than the same material of a darker value.
7 All colours, with the exception of black, are capable of reflecting some light. Light colours, e.g. white, yellow, pink, yellow-green and yellow-orange reflect more light than darker ones, e.g. dark blue, dark green and dark red.

Light behaves in a predictable way and, because it affects everything we see, it must be the starting point for an understanding of drawing, rendering and painting..

15

12 An automatic aperture preferred 35mm single lens reflex camera, the Contax RTS. This is one of a number of high-quality 35mm SLR cameras of this type available from various manufacturers, e.g. Leica, Nikon, Canon, Olympus, Yashica, etc. The camera is an instrument which uses light to produce 'mechanical renderings' and can be of enormous value in the process of understanding light.

Photographs, which can be considered to be mechanical renderings, can be of enormous value in developing an understanding of light and how it is recorded in two-dimensional representations of three-dimensional objects or views.

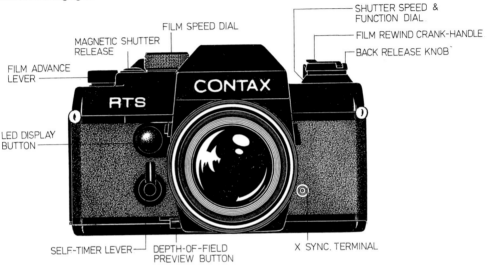

SHUTTER SPEED & FUNCTION DIAL

FILM SPEED DIAL

FILM REWIND CRANK-HANDLE

MAGNETIC SHUTTER RELEASE

BACK RELEASE KNOB

FILM ADVANCE LEVER

LED DISPLAY BUTTON

SELF-TIMER LEVER

DEPTH-OF-FIELD PREVIEW BUTTON

X SYNC. TERMINAL

FRONT VIEW

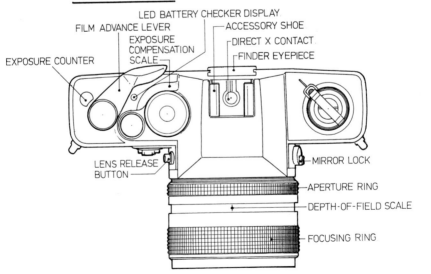

LED BATTERY CHECKER DISPLAY

FILM ADVANCE LEVER

ACCESSORY SHOE

EXPOSURE COMPENSATION SCALE

DIRECT X CONTACT

FINDER EYEPIECE

EXPOSURE COUNTER

LENS RELEASE BUTTON

MIRROR LOCK

APERTURE RING

DEPTH-OF-FIELD SCALE

FOCUSING RING

TOP VIEW

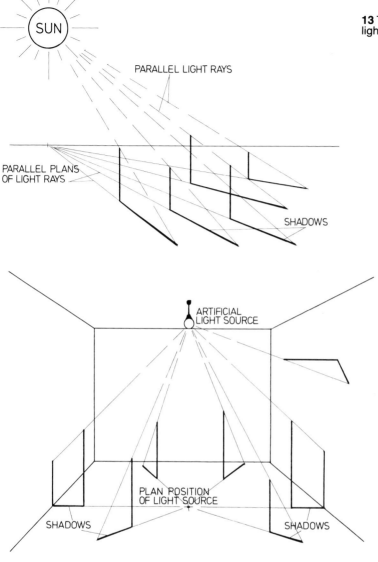

SUN

PARALLEL LIGHT RAYS

PARALLEL PLANS OF LIGHT RAYS

SHADOWS

ARTIFICIAL LIGHT SOURCE

PLAN POSITION OF LIGHT SOURCE

SHADOWS

SHADOWS

Light rays from the sun and artificial light sources differ in only one respect: light rays from the sun travel in straight, parallel lines, whereas light rays from a simple, artificial light source radiate from a point (**13**). Though it is fairly obvious that light rays radiate from the sun, because of the limited areas involved in most pictorial projects the divergence from parallel of the sun's light rays is so infinitesimal that it can safely be ignored by artists and delineators. This knowledge that light rays from the sun are straight and parallel enables shadow shapes to be set up in perspective constructions using the normal basic principles of perspective projection.

As it becomes necessary these aspects of light will be explained more fully.

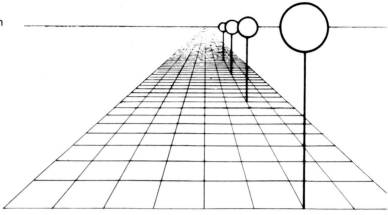

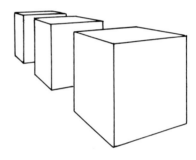

Basic optical laws

Of equal importance to an understanding of the behaviour
of light is an understanding of the basic optical laws, which
include perspective, light and shade, and atmospheric effect.
Each of these three main elements produces a number of
effects, which are discussed as they become necessary to a
complete understanding of the overall subject.

The three most important elements of perspective are:
1 Convergence 2 Diminution and 3 Foreshortening (**14,
15**).

1 As parallel lines recede from the observer they appear to
come closer together at a constant rate. This is known as
convergence.

2 Objects of the same size appear to become smaller as the
distance between them and the observer increases. This is
known as diminution.

3 Equal spaces between objects appear to become shorter at
a constant rate as the distance between them and the
observer increases. This is known as foreshortening.

Perspective projection is the method of combining convergence, diminution and foreshortening to produce an accurate line drawing of the shape of an object or view, which can be rendered to produce a pictorial representation. Because each part of perspective projection is based on optical facts, i.e. is consistent with what is seen when viewing the object itself, an accurate shape of an object or view can be produced.

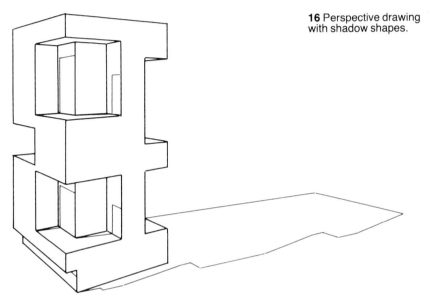

16 Perspective drawing with shadow shapes.

Any drawing that is to form the basis for a rendering must have shadow shapes added to the perspective drawing before it can be considered complete (**16**).

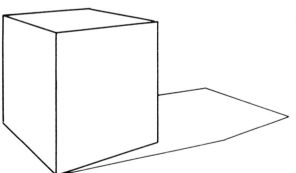

17 Perspective drawing of a cube with shadow shape.

Shadow-shape constructions are simple extensions of basic perspective projections in which inclined parallel lines (light rays) and their plans are used (**17**). (See *Basic Perspective* and *Creative Perspective* for full explanations of perspective and shadow-shape constructions.)

18 A typical mistake made in architectural rendering.

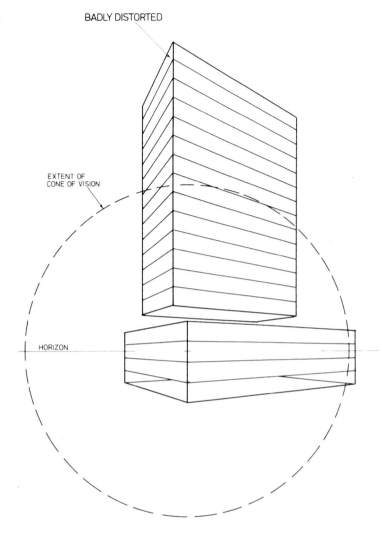

The cone of vision and the one-look principle

The cone of vision and the one-look principle are two very important aspects of perspective projection which are frequently disregarded. This is responsible for some very unfortunate distortions which are particularly noticeable in architectural renderings.

The illustration (**18**) shows one of the most common mistakes made when the one-look principle and the cone of vision are ignored.

In perspective drawing, as in still photography, the observer is limited to what is known as the one-look principle. This means that for the purpose of making a picture the observer's eyes must be perfectly still at the moment of looking at the subject. This is because the drawing (or photograph) will be a single image seen from a specific viewing position at a specific moment in time and this single image

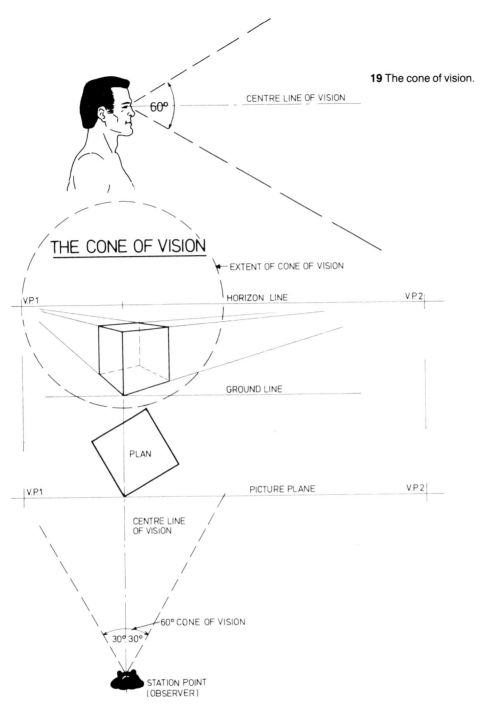

19 The cone of vision.

CENTRE LINE OF VISION

60°

THE CONE OF VISION

EXTENT OF CONE OF VISION

V.P.1   HORIZON LINE   V.P.2

GROUND LINE

PLAN

V.P.1   PICTURE PLANE   V.P.2

CENTRE LINE
OF VISION

60° CONE OF VISION

30° 30°

STATION POINT
(OBSERVER)

does not allow for movement on the part of the observer's eyes (or the camera lens), nor of any element within the picture. The photographer is aware that his camera must be perfectly still at the moment he presses the shutter-release or the result will be not a single image but a blurred picture, for he will get more than one image on his negative. If he wants his photograph to cover a greater area, he must move further away from the subject so that his camera lens will record a greater area.

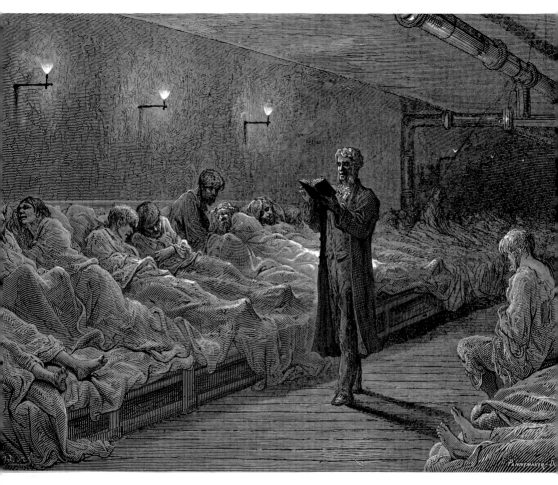

20 In his engraving of a *Bible-reading in a Night Refuge*, Gustave Doré has recorded a dramatic moment in a single image that 'his eye saw clearly when it was held still'.

When making a drawing the artist must record only the single image that his eyes can see clearly when they are perfectly still like the camera lens. Because the human eye is limited in the area it can see when it is perfectly still, this limit, known as the cone of vision, must be used by the artist to control the amount of the subject to be included in the picture in the same way as a photographer uses the viewfinder of a camera. If this limit of the cone of vision is ignored, as was shown in the illustration of the multistorey building (**18**), distortions of the image will result. The solution to this often-seen fault is to move the station point (the position of the observer's eye) on the basic perspective construction further back from the subject.

For all pictorial representations, the maximum cone of vision of the human eye is accepted as sixty degrees. The perspective construction (**19**) illustrates how the cone of vision is used to check that the whole of the required subject will be undistorted in the final picture. Remember that the cone of vision is three-dimensional and so the height as well as the plan of the object must be checked with the cone of vision.

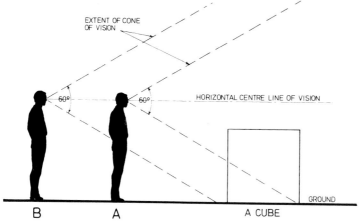

Observer 'A' (**21**) is shown standing too close to the object for a satisfactory picture of the whole of it to be made. If he moves back to position 'B' the whole of the height of the object falls within his static cone of vision and a picture of the whole of the object can be made without unacceptable distortions.

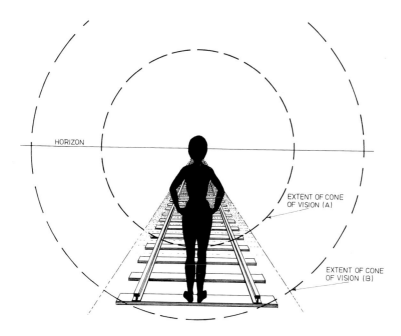

The moving of the viewing position to increase the area covered by the cone of vision is further demonstrated in this illustration (**22**). The limit of the cone of vision (A) for the observer shown standing on the railroad track is indicated, together with the limit of the cone of vision (B) of the artist making the picture of this situation. Obviously the artist is standing directly behind the observer he has drawn, is using the same eye-level and is looking in the same direction.

When the one-look principle and the cone of vision are understood, they can be used to control the limits of a picture and thus eliminate unfortunate distortions which may otherwise occur, even though all of the other aspects of a perspective construction may have been used correctly. One final point is that the wise renderer always tries to place the subject well within the cone of vision. Whilst it is admitted that this is sometimes difficult in interior renderings where space is limited and it is necessary to work to the absolute limits of the cone of vision, an experienced renderer working with extreme care can produce a satisfactory result.

23 Three examples of a cube.

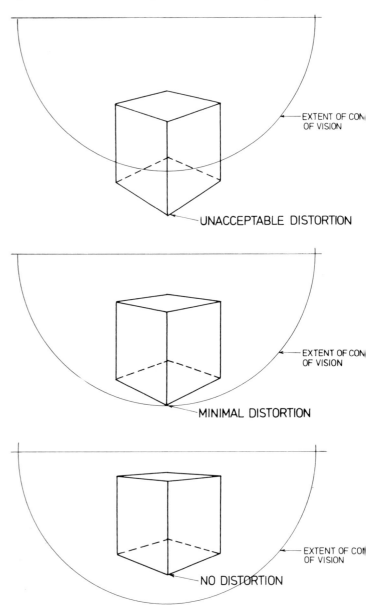

EXTENT OF CON OF VISION

UNACCEPTABLE DISTORTION

EXTENT OF CON OF VISION

MINIMAL DISTORTION

EXTENT OF CON OF VISION

NO DISTORTION

This group of three illustrations (23) shows the difference in the view of the critical, lower-front corner of a cube placed in differing relationships to the limit of the cone of vision.

The first example shows the unacceptable distortion of the lower-front corner of the cube when it falls outside the limit of the cone of vision.

The second example shows the cube drawn within but at the very limit of the cone of vision. Whilst it cannot be claimed to be unacceptably distorted, it can easily be seen that the third example, which is well inside the limits of the cone of vision, is preferable to the second. Naturally, informed judgment is required when considering the placement of an object or objects within the picture area.

In (18) the unfortunate distortion at the top of the building could have been avoided by placing the whole building within the cone of vision. An external view of a right angle, as in the closest corner of the building, can never appear as an angle of less than ninety degrees.

The advantages of avoiding the extreme limits of the cone of vision should be obvious. When it is necessary to work to these limits, do so with great care and never go beyond them.

Atmospheric effect

Atmospheric effect is one of the most important optical effects because, like perspective and light and shade, it affects everything that is seen. In rendering it is essential to understand and use it correctly.

24 Francesco Guardi has used atmospheric effect to create the illusion of depth in this rendering of the Piazza di San Marco, Venice.

25 a–d Atmospheric effect.

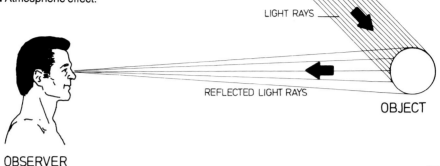

LIGHT RAYS

REFLECTED LIGHT RAYS

OBJECT

OBSERVER

25a

The sun's rays strike the object and are reflected through the intervening space in such a way that they are registered by the observer's eye (**25a**). If the intervening space is clear, i.e. has no obstructions, the light rays can travel uninterrupted in a direct line and the observer will see a strong, bright, clear image of the object.

ATMOSPHERIC POLLUTION

OBSERVER

25b

The air on our planet has in it many natural as well as man-made pollutants in the form of solids of various kinds as well as other materials, such as water particles, all of which are capable of reflecting or deflecting light rays even though they are individually very small (**25b**).

Without becoming involved in exactly what many of these pollutants are, it is sufficient to understand that particles of dust, which are in evidence everywhere, are suspended in the air and are solids capable of reflecting light rays. If the dust particles are dense enough, as in a dust storm, they can completely block the observer's view of an object even at a comparatively short distance. Similarly, a really heavy fog can virtually stop the sun's light rays from reaching an object with the inevitable result that the observer cannot see it. Heavy smoke can also block an observer's view of an object as can, to a greater or lesser extent, heavy rain.

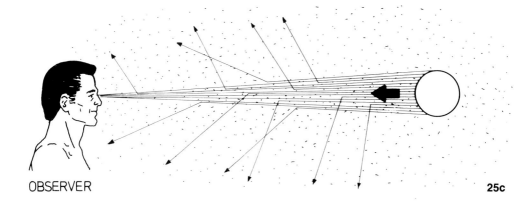

OBSERVER   **25c**

Under normal circumstances these pollutants are present in varying proportions in our atmosphere. The light rays reflected from an object must travel through the atmosphere with all of its tiny, solid, opaque particles of various pollutants before they reach the observer's eye. (**25c**). That some of these reflected light rays will strike solids suspended in the atmosphere and be deflected from their true course to the observer's eye is inevitable. It necessarily follows that if the number of light rays reaching the observer's eye is reduced, the seen image of the object must be reduced in intensity, brightness and clarity. Therefore, if the object is closer to the observer's eye, the light rays will have to pass through less atmosphere and fewer of them will chance deflection from their course by colliding with solid particles of some pollutant.

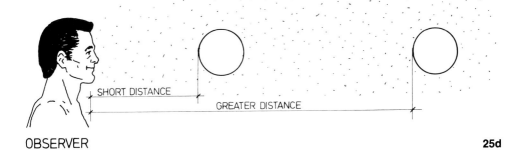

SHORT DISTANCE

GREATER DISTANCE

OBSERVER   **25d**

The result of placing the object close to the observer's eye will be a clear, intense and bright image of the object seen by that observer (**25d**). As the distance increases, atmospheric effect will result in a less clear, less intense and less bright image being seen by the observer.

The result of this atmospheric effect can be readily seen or photographed and, because atmospheric effect is evident in almost everything seen, it is an important factor in producing an accurate image.

26 Five spheres placed to demonstrate the effect of atmosphere.

This illustration (**26**) of five identical spheres placed at different distances from an observer demonstrates how atmospheric effect influences what is seen by that observer. The drawing shows how the values, i.e. degrees of darkness and lightness, are reduced as the distance increases. The dark areas tend to become less dark and the light areas tend to become less light. This reduction of contrast causes the observer to see a reduction of image intensity as the distance increases. If more identical spheres were placed even further away from the observer, the furthest ones would be very hard to see clearly, distinguishing their different values would be almost impossible and it might even be difficult to recognize them as spheres.

27 A landscape showing atmospheric effect. Values in the foreground are strongly contrasted and because of atmospheric effect reduce as the distance increases.

This effect can be seen in the photograph (**27**) in which the values in the foreground are strongly contrasted. As the distance from the camera increases, these contrasts are reduced until they are virtually neutralized; they no longer have different values and, therefore, no contrast exists between them.

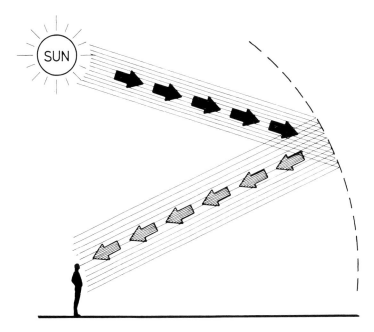

28 Diagrammatic explanation of the atmospheric umbrella.

Atmospheric effect is not limited to the deflection of reflected light rays travelling between an object and an observer's eye. It also has a considerable effect on the appearance of an object because it affects the values seen on the surfaces of that object. The pollutants suspended in the atmosphere form a sort of umbrella, which is capable of reflecting light rays as they travel from the sun in such a way that they make the sky look very bright, even when the observer has his back towards the sun (**28**). This phenomenon can only be the result of some form of effective reflector suspended in the atmosphere and can easily be verified by observation.

If there is no effective reflector in the atmosphere, as is the case on the moon, the observer will see a black sky (**29**, overleaf). To see a light sky, light rays must be reflected in the direction of the observer's eye from something tiny, which must be present in the atmosphere in very large quantities. In the earth's atmosphere this something is the pollutants, which act as tiny light reflectors.

29 The lack of atmosphere on the surface of the moon means that it has no effective reflectors for light rays, therefore the sky looks black.

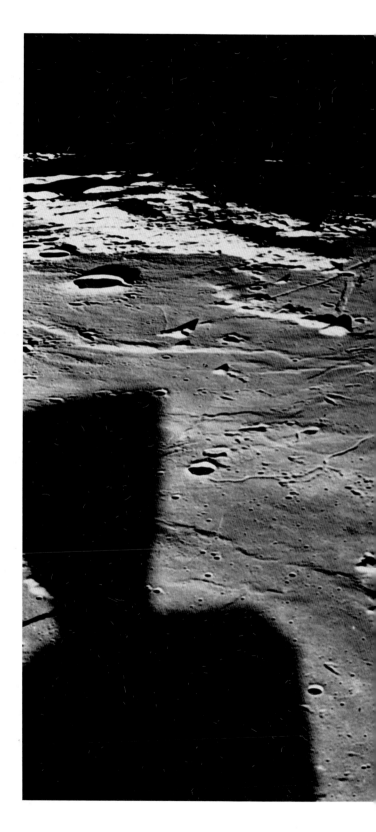

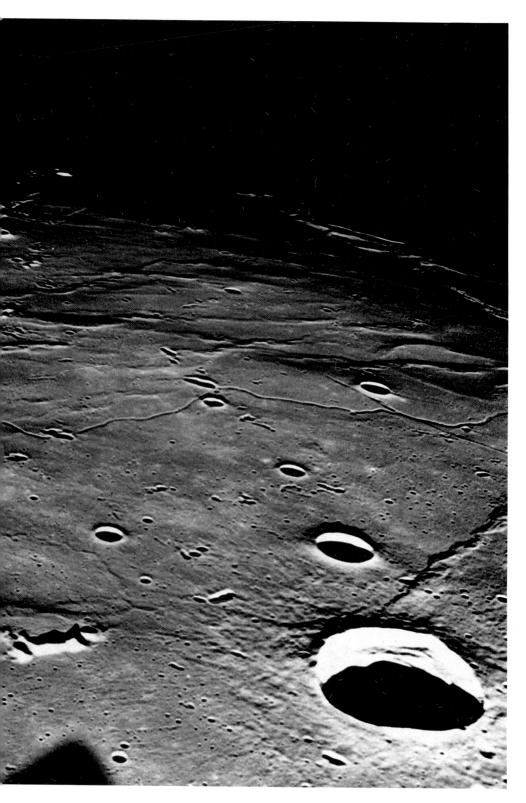

30 Mirror demonstration.

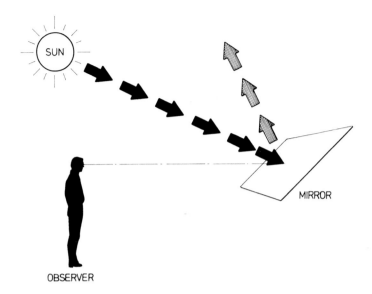

It has been my experience that many students have considerable difficulty with this concept of the eye being able to see only objects which reflect light rays in such a way that they can be registered on the retina of the eye. Many believe that if light strikes an object it will be seen but this is not necessarily so. For example, if an object is placed so that the light rays striking it are reflected away from the observer's eye, as shown in the illustration (30), the observer will see nothing.

If the object is a mirror (the most efficient reflector) and the condition shown is located in space, which is outside the earth's atmosphere and its atmospheric umbrella, the observer will be totally unaware of the mirror's existence.

31 Mirror demonstration with object.

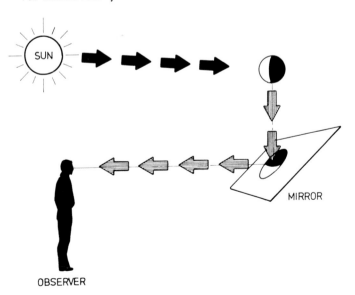

If a simple object is introduced in a particular location, the observer will see the object because the light rays are striking it and some of them are being reflected by the mirror back in the direction of the observer's eye (31). Though the observer still cannot see the mirror, he will see in the mirror the reflection of this carefully placed object (32). The object has been placed to take advantage of the fact that the angle of reflection equals the angle of incidence of a light ray.

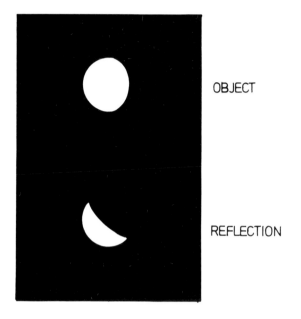

32 What the observer sees.

OBJECT

REFLECTION

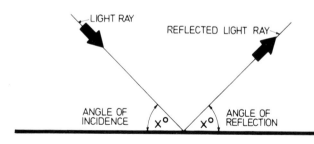

LIGHT RAY

REFLECTED LIGHT RAY

ANGLE OF INCIDENCE $x°$

$x°$ ANGLE OF REFLECTION

33 The angle of reflection equals the angle of incidence of a light ray.

Physics establishes that the angle of reflection of a light ray equals its angle of incidence (33). It is this fact that enables us to follow light rays and calculate their behaviour regarding seen images.

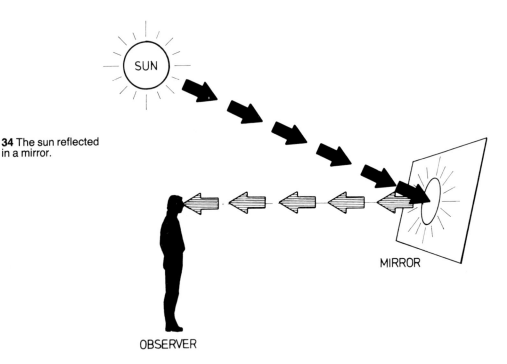

34 The sun reflected in a mirror.

MIRROR

OBSERVER

If the same mirror had its angle to the observer's centre line of vision altered slightly, the observer would no longer see the reflection of the object in the mirror but would see a reflection of the sun, the light source (**34**). In the examples used so far the observer could not have seen the mirror, regardless of the strength of light involved. It is not the number or strength of the light rays striking an object that enables it to be seen, but its ability to reflect light rays in the direction of the observer's eye.

35 The sky reflected in a mirror.

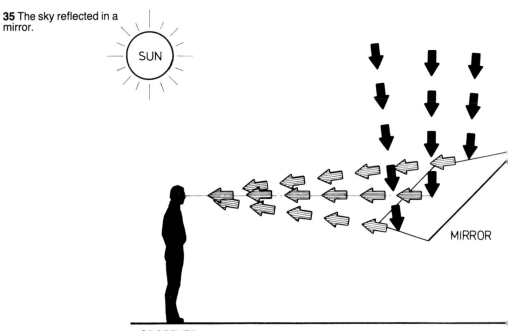

MIRROR

OBSERVER

When this observer/mirror relationship is moved from outer space to the surface of the earth, the light rays from the sun will still strike the mirror and be reflected away from the observer's eye. On this evidence he should not be able to see the mirror, but practical experiment proves that he can see it (35). Because the mirror can be seen, light rays are obviously being reflected towards the observer's eye. If these reflected light rays responsible for his seeing the mirror are followed, using the knowledge that the angle of reflection of light rays is equal to their angle of incidence, it is possible to locate their source, which in this case is the atmospheric umbrella in conjunction with the sun.

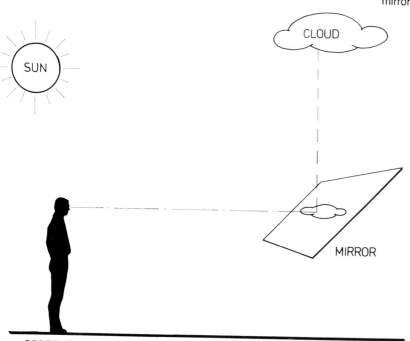

36 A cloud reflected in a mirror.

CLOUD

SUN

MIRROR

OBSERVER

If the area of the sky (atmospheric umbrella) contains any object such as a cloud, the observer will see the mirror and also the reflection of the cloud (36).

When it is understood that seeing occurs because light rays are reflected towards the eye, not because light strikes an object, even though both must happen for an object to be seen, it is possible to understand that surfaces in different positions can reflect light rays towards the observer's eye with varying degrees of efficiency, which result in tonal variation.

Under normal circumstances, horizontal surfaces seen in light appear lighter than vertical surfaces seen under the same conditions, e.g. a table top and edge, a simple cube, etc. This is clearly demonstrated in the photograph (37), particularly where the horizontal and vertical surfaces are of the same material, value and colour. It is important to understand the principles and be able to use them in pictorial representation, where the illusion of the third dimension often relies heavily on correct tonal values.

Direct light rays from the sun strike the various surfaces of this object (38) and their reflection will be directed away from the observer. Those striking the vertical surface are reflected down to the horizontal plane in front of the vertical plane, and from there are reflected towards the observer's eye. Therefore it is this horizontal plane, not the vertical plane, which is reflecting more light rays towards the observer's eye. The result is that the horizontal plane will appear lighter to him because it reflects more light rays in his direction.

37 Tonal variation on horizontal and vertical surfaces. Under normal lighting conditions the top horizontal surface will appear lighter than a vertical surface in light.

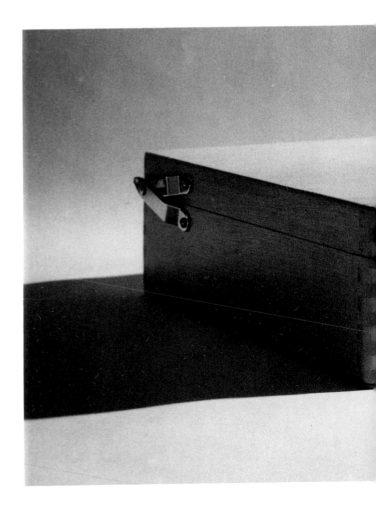

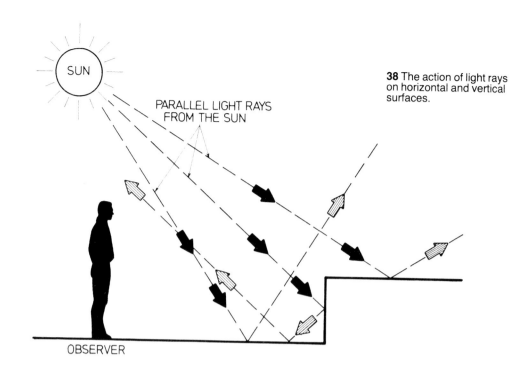

SUN

PARALLEL LIGHT RAYS
FROM THE SUN

38 The action of light rays
on horizontal and vertical
surfaces.

OBSERVER

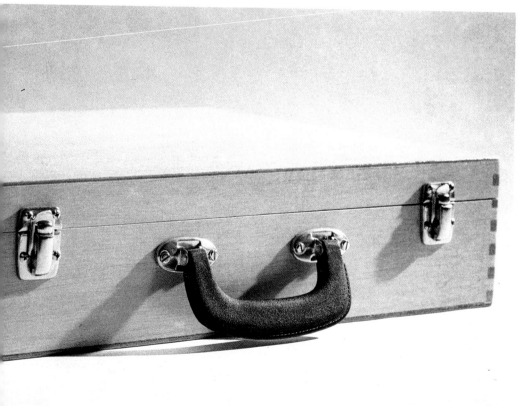

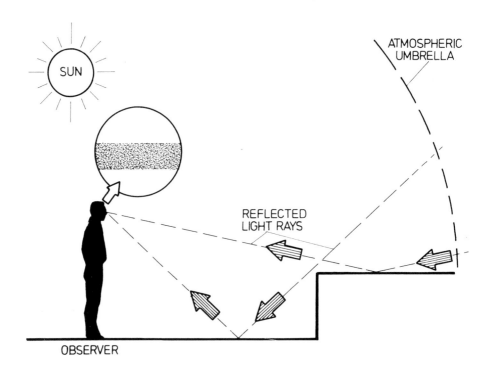

39 The effect of the atmospheric umbrella.

40 A more complex arrangement of horizontal and vertical planes.

If the atmospheric umbrella is understood, it will be seen that the light rays reflected from it are directed to the horizontal surfaces at which the observer is looking (**39**). (Only those light rays directly involved in what the observer sees are shown.) They strike the horizontal surfaces, which become very efficient reflectors of light rays in the direction

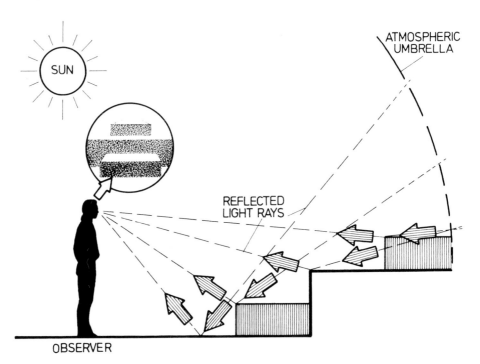

of the observer. The vertical surface, even though it is receiving the same amount of direct sunlight as the horizontal surfaces, is receiving no useful light from the atmospheric umbrella as far as this observer is concerned. The observer will see the horizontal surfaces as lighter values than the vertical one because they are reflecting more light in the direction of his eye.

If more horizontal and vertical planes are added, the results seen by the observer will remain consistent and he will see the horizontal surfaces as lighter values than the vertical ones (40). Observation will confirm that under all normal conditions this will always be so. In this context, 'normal conditions' means that no extraneous reflections are allowed to interfere with the object being observed.

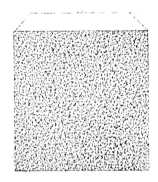

41 A rendered cube – a one-point construction.

The fact that under normal conditions horizontal surfaces will always appear lighter than vertical surfaces seen in the same light is of enormous value to the renderer. Using this information he can clearly establish the change of direction between horizontal and vertical surfaces seen in light (41).

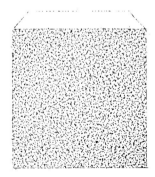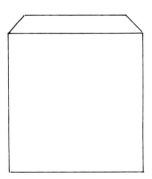

42 A comparison of a rendered and an unrendered cube.

This illustration (42) shows how the introduction of this change of value on the vertical and horizontal surfaces in the rendered example gives a greater illusion of a third dimension, because the variation between the two surfaces is consistent with optical reality. The example on the right does not have this evidence of optical reality and is somewhat ambiguous.

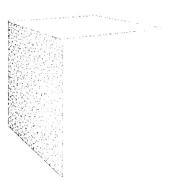

A static plane is one that is seen at right angles to the observer's centre line of vision. A dynamic plane is one that is seen at an angle other than a right angle to the observer's centre line of vision (**43**). In all the examples shown so far, all the vertical surfaces seen in light have been static planes, which have been completely shielded from any effective reflected light rays from the atmospheric umbrella. This shielding causes the difference in value between the vertical and horizontal surfaces to be considerable. In fact, under these circumstances the difference will be the greatest seen by the observer, because as the vertical surface is rotated on its vertical axis it will obviously become increasingly affected by light rays reflected by the atmospheric umbrella. The result will be a slight lightening of the value seen by the observer.

Though the reflected light rays from the atmospheric umbrella will, for the most part, be reflected downwards to the base plane, others from the lower part of the atmospheric umbrella could be directed in the general direction of the observer's eye. Some surfaces, particularly the ground plane and others very near it, could reflect light rays which would strike the angled vertical plane and be reflected towards the observer's eye. Even a small increase in the amount of reflected light will affect the value seen by the observer, but under normal conditions the amount of light reflected by dynamic vertical surfaces will not equal that reflected by horizontal surfaces.

As the height of the vertical plane increases it will reflect more light rays from the atmospheric umbrella towards the observer's eye (**44**).

The observer sees the vertical plane as a dynamic surface of graduated value with the darkest value at the lowest part. As the height increases, the value becomes lighter, because the surface becomes more efficient in its ability to reflect light rays in the direction of the observer's eye (**45**).

When this principle is applied to a number of identical cubes placed one above the other, the value on the vertical surfaces seen in light will be darkest on the lowest one and will become progressively lighter as the height increases (**46**).

44 A dynamic vertical plane extended in height.

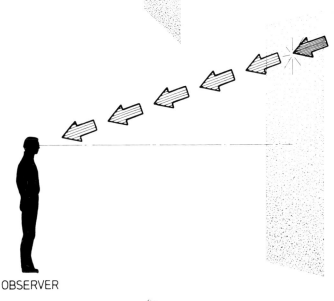

FROM ATMOSPHERIC UMBRELLA

OBSERVER

45 An explanation of a vertical plane extended in height.

46 An open stack of cubes.

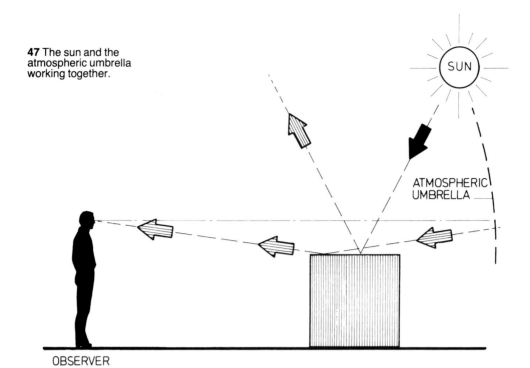

47 The sun and the atmospheric umbrella working together.

SUN

ATMOSPHERIC UMBRELLA

OBSERVER

The sun can, under certain circumstances, supply the light rays which are directed towards the observer's eye. However, these cases are rare and usually when it might at first appear to the inexperienced person that the sun itself is responsible, it is more often than not the atmospheric umbrella working in conjunction with the sun which is responsible. The illustration (**47**) shows how this may happen when the sun is in front of the observer instead of behind him, as it has been in the previous examples.

The conditions illustrated are by no means all of the possibilities likely to be encountered, but the principles remain the same for all situations. If the reflected light rays and their source are located, the image seen by an observer can be logically reasoned and a convincing pictorial representation made even if the object exists only in the imagination.

The atmospheric umbrella, being three-dimensional, is all round an observer, not just in front of him, but the illustration (**48**) shows it only in plan and at a much reduced scale. The observer has his back to the sun and he is surrounded by atmosphere, all of which is capable of reflecting light rays because of the pollutants suspended in it. This means that the atmosphere is capable of reflecting light rays in all directions and as a result the observer will see its effect, no matter which way he looks.

In spite of this the area behind the observer will normally have only a minimal effect on what he sees, whilst the rest of the atmospheric umbrella will have considerable, direct effect on what he sees when he looks in one specific direction (**49**).

42

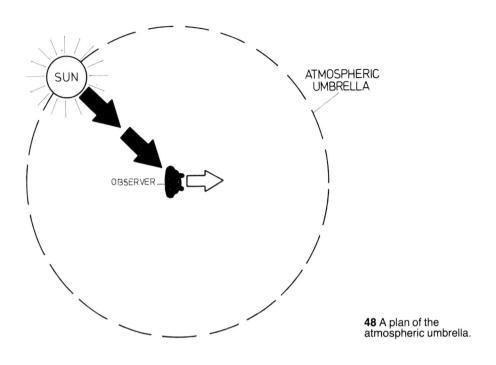

48 A plan of the atmospheric umbrella.

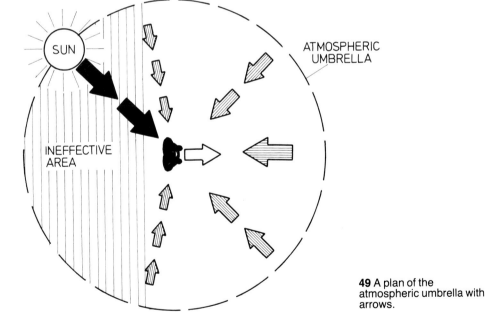

49 A plan of the atmospheric umbrella with arrows.

50 An observer looking in the direction of the sun.

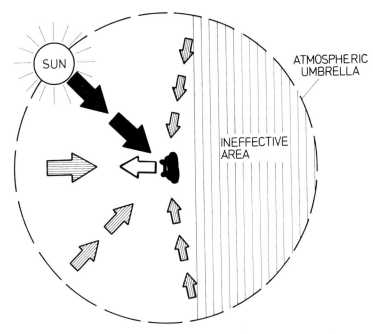

ATMOSPHERIC UMBRELLA

INEFFECTIVE AREA

SUN

If the observer in the previous illustration is rotated through 180 degrees, so that he is now looking in the general direction of the light source, i.e. the sun, the area behind him will again have little direct effect on what he sees, whilst the rest of the atmospheric umbrella will contribute directly to what he sees (50).

If the elevation and plan are considered together, it can be understood how light rays reflected from a larger area of the atmospheric umbrella would be capable of affecting what the observer sees (51). The extent of the atmospheric umbrella is extremely important and the student is advised to neither underestimate nor overestimate its effect on what is seen. In rendering, a simple diagram of the conditions can often help when problems are encountered.

51 An elevation of atmospheric effect.

ATMOSPHERIC UMBRELLA

SUN

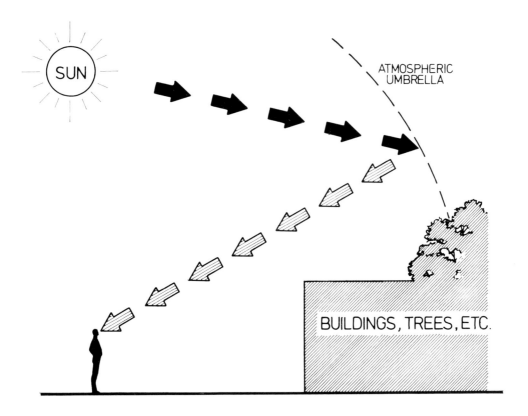

SUN

ATMOSPHERIC
UMBRELLA

BUILDINGS, TREES, ETC.

The loss of efficiency of the atmospheric umbrella as it nears the ground frequently interferes with what is seen. Often buildings, trees, hills, mountains, etc. are located behind the object being observed and, though these objects are capable of reflecting light rays, they are seldom as efficient as the atmospheric umbrella. The illustration (52) shows a diagrammatic explanation of this condition. Remember that the buildings will reflect light rays down towards the ground rather than towards the eye of the observer, and note how the effectiveness of the atmospheric umbrella is totally destroyed towards the ground. Also, the faces of the buildings seen by the observer are in full sunlight, for the sun's rays are striking them directly, but these light rays from the sun are directed downwards to the ground, not towards the observer's eye. However, the part of the atmospheric umbrella that is behind the buildings is very bright and is reflecting light rays towards the observer's eye. The result is that, in a sense, the faces of the buildings seen by the observer will be in shade, not from the sun, because they face the sun's location, but from the atmospheric umbrella, which is a secondary light source. This condition, described as being in shade from the atmospheric umbrella, must not be confused with what is usually meant by the term shade. Shade exists when a face of an object is turned away from a light source.

52 An elevation of buildings and trees.

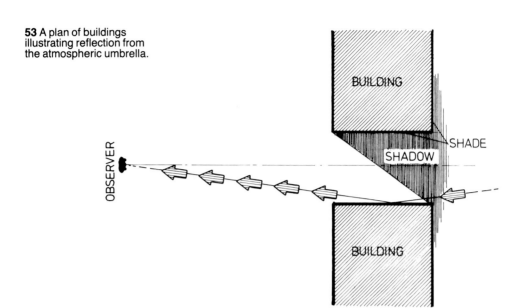

53 A plan of buildings illustrating reflection from the atmospheric umbrella.

OBSERVER

BUILDING

SHADE

SHADOW

BUILDING

The sun is the light source in this illustration (53), so the faces of the buildings which are turned away from the sun will be in shade. As previously mentioned, the static faces of the buildings at which the observer is looking will be slightly darker than a side wall seen in light, because a side wall will be in a position where it will probably reflect some light from the atmospheric umbrella towards the observer's eye. This particular aspect of surfaces in various locations with regard to the atmospheric umbrella is discussed in more detail later.

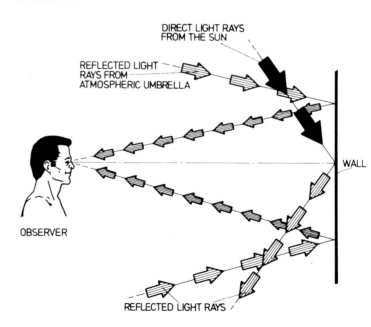

54 An observer looking at a wall.

DIRECT LIGHT RAYS FROM THE SUN

REFLECTED LIGHT RAYS FROM ATMOSPHERIC UMBRELLA

WALL

OBSERVER

REFLECTED LIGHT RAYS

The final aspect of surfaces seen in light to be examined at this stage is the actual surface itself. As has been established, when light rays from the sun, or any light source, strike a surface they are reflected in accordance with the principle, 'The angle of reflection equals the angle of incidence of a light ray.' This means that, in general, a surface seen in light will reflect light rays in one direction only. In theory this is so, but in practice other factors must also be considered. For example, if the surface is seen in direct sunlight, as shown in the illustration (54), the light rays will be directed down towards the ground plane and not towards the observer's eye. Theoretically, the observer will not be able to see the vertical surface, but practical observation shows that under these conditions the vertical surface can be seen. The reason for this is the presence of reflected light from various surfaces around the one under consideration and from the atmospheric umbrella. This is even more easily understood when it is realized that a perfectly smooth reflecting surface is extremely rare and, if such a thing actually did exist, it would seldom be seen under perfect conditions, i.e. free of imperfections and without dust or other pollutants adhering to it.

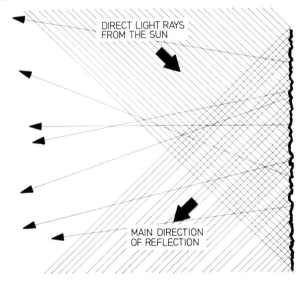

DIRECT LIGHT RAYS FROM THE SUN

MAIN DIRECTION OF REFLECTION

55 An uneven vertical surface.

The illustration of the wall magnified many times (55) shows how these imperfections and pollutants are capable of reflecting light rays in directions other than the main one, which is down towards the ground plane. From this it can be seen how some of the light rays would inevitably be reflected in the direction of the observer's eye. Though it is acknowledged that the light rays reflected from the surface imperfections would probably not be as numerous as those from the overall surface, they would be considerable and would therefore add to the lightness of the surface being seen.

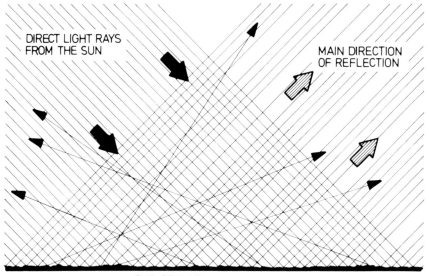

DIRECT LIGHT RAYS
FROM THE SUN

MAIN DIRECTION
OF REFLECTION

THE GROUND

56 The ground plane.

The ground plane is probably the best example of this particular aspect of light reflection. Though the ground is a generally flat plane (56), it consists of many fine particles of various shapes such as pebbles, stones and dust, each of which is capable of reflecting light rays in other than the main direction for the ground plane (57).

The main direction of the reflected light rays will be at an angle equal to that formed by the light rays striking the generally flat ground plane, but it can easily be seen that every individual stone, pebble, and particle of dust has changes of direction on its surface. Each of their tiny surfaces is capable of reflecting light rays in a multitude of different directions.

57 The ground magnified.

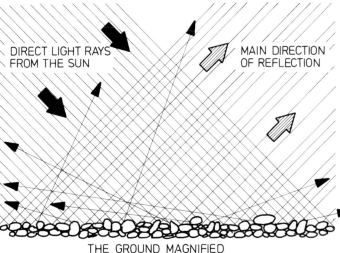

DIRECT LIGHT RAYS
FROM THE SUN

MAIN DIRECTION
OF REFLECTION

THE GROUND MAGNIFIED

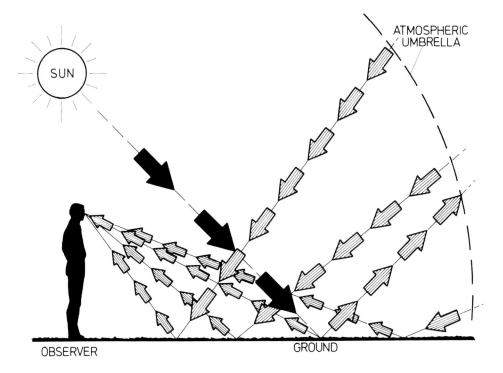

SUN

ATMOSPHERIC
UMBRELLA

OBSERVER

GROUND

Wherever the observer looks at the ground, some of the light rays reflected from these small surfaces will inevitably be directed towards his eye (58). They, together with the reflected light rays from the atmospheric umbrella and those from the sun, are the reason an observer can see the ground plane so clearly in normal sunlight, no matter where he stands in relation to the sun.

The way light is reflected by different surfaces in various positions has a direct link with the way they are seen and with the way they are rendered if the illusion of reality is to be produced. Therefore, a sound understanding of the basic principles of light reflection is one of the most important areas of fundamental knowledge for students, irrespective of the area of art, design or graphics they may wish to enter.

The foregoing information is intended as a direction for the student to pursue rather than a catalogue of effects for use in rendering. The camera can be of considerable value in gathering knowledge in this as well as other areas of study.

58 An observer looking at the ground.

59 The sun is behind the photographer, as indicated by the shadows, but because the white building is acting as a reflecting surface, i.e. it replaces the atmospheric umbrella, the vertical face of the kerb is darker than the horizontal surface.

The value of photographic evidence becomes clear upon examining this picture of a road and pavement (59), which illustrates some very interesting effects. Note the darker value of the vertical face of the kerb, even though it is in sun-

light, as is evidenced by the shadow of the small tree and the face of the building. Much can be learned by carefully examining photographs of even rather commonplace subjects such as this one.

Shade and shadow

In considering shade and shadow much of the previous information about light reflection is relevant. For example, shade and shadow areas are usually exposed, at least to some degree, to light rays from the atmospheric umbrella. By definition, shade and shadow have certain relationships to the light source inasmuch as the direct light rays cannot reach them. Because of the importance of a complete under-

standing of shade and shadow their definitions are essential, so that each condition is not confused with the other.

Shade exists when a surface is turned away from a light source.

Shadow exists when an opaque object is placed between a light source and a surface on which the light would normally fall.

60 In this watercolour stage design for a prison, Giuseppe Galli Bibiena uses light and shade to introduce a superb feeling of reality into this theatrical setting.

61 A rendered cube.

If this simple cube is examined it will be seen that some of its surfaces are seen in light and some are seen in shade (**61**). The cube also casts a shadow on the ground plane and, as expected, this shadow is in the opposite direction to the light source. To understand how the surfaces in shade and shadow must be rendered to produce the illusion of reality, it is necessary to understand if and how they will be affected by reflected light rays. To do this it is necessary to examine the conditions under which the cube is being viewed.

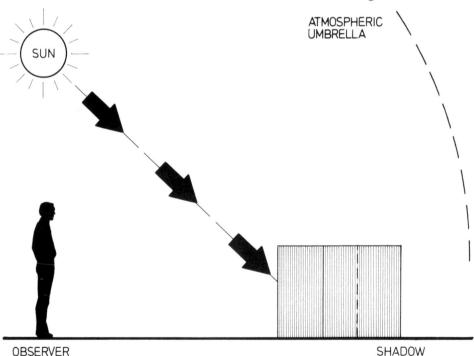

62 An observer looking at a cube.

The observer (**62**) is placed so that he will see the cube as it was illustrated in (**61**). The location of the sun is indicated, as is the atmospheric umbrella. The observer can see only one surface of the cube in shade, so it is necessary to consider only this side. (Two vertical sides will be in light and two will be in shade.) If only the direct light rays from the sun are considered, it can be seen that they have no effect on the shade and shadow areas.

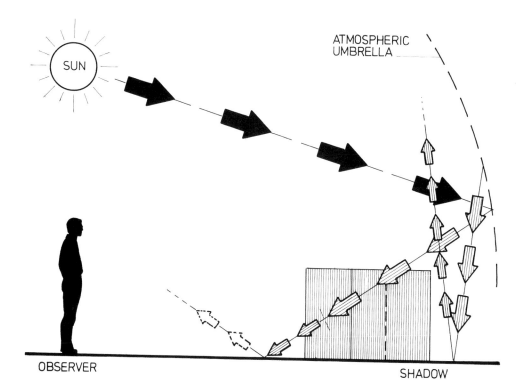

SUN

ATMOSPHERIC UMBRELLA

OBSERVER

SHADOW

In this diagram (63) the reflected light rays from the atmospheric umbrella are shown with their direct reflections, none of which is directed towards the observer's eye. Those light rays from the atmospheric umbrella that do strike the surface in shade are directed to the ground plane and are of little use to the illustrated observer. Those that strike the shadow on the horizontal ground plane are reflected back up into the sky and are of no value to this observer.

Observation shows that the shade area of an object, seen under normal conditions, is a little lighter in value than the shadow area. The reason for this is that the shade area is receiving more reflected light, which is directed back to the observer's eye, than is the shadow area. The source of this extra light reflection from the shade area is shown in the next diagram.

63 Shade and shadow unaffected by the atmospheric umbrella.

55

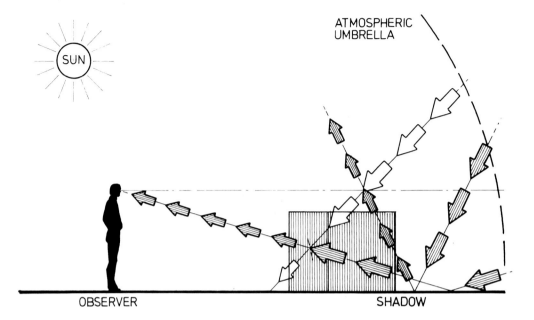

SUN

ATMOSPHERIC
UMBRELLA

OBSERVER

SHADOW

64 Reflection into the
shade area.

By following the light rays from the atmospheric umbrella it can be seen how those striking the horizontal shadow area are almost all reflected back up into the sky, so that they are virtually useless to the observer (**64**). Whilst it is true that some few light rays will be directed from the shadow area towards the observer (otherwise it would look completely black to him), they are very few and so he sees a very dark value. Because the shade area is a vertical plane, the light rays from the atmospheric umbrella will strike it and be directed downwards to the ground plane and from there back up into the sky. This is of little value to the observer. However, some of the light rays from the atmospheric umbrella striking the ground behind the object will be reflected into the shade area and from there to the observer's eye. This causes the shade area to appear a little lighter in value than the horizontal shadow area. The actual value seen will vary with the effectiveness of the source of the reflected light rays which strike the shade area but obviously, the more light rays directed to the observer's eye, the lighter the shade area will appear.

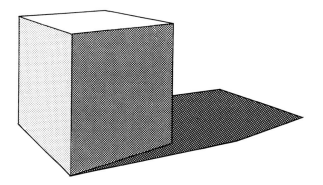

The basic tonal pattern

From the preceding information it is possible to show on a drawing of a cube and its shadow the relationship of the various tonal values of the surfaces seen by an observer looking at the actual cube (65). Under normal conditions, the top horizontal plane in light will be the lightest value seen on the cube, and the vertical plane in light will be slightly darker than the horizontal plane but still a light value. The vertical plane seen in shade will be the darkest value seen on the cube and the shadow on the horizontal ground plane will be the darkest value in the drawing. This simple diagram illustrates what is known as the 'basic tonal pattern' and it remains valid for the vertical and horizontal planes of all objects seen under normal conditions.

The basic tonal pattern can be developed with more complex shapes including two additional, frequently found conditions, which are a shade on an underside of an object or part of an object, and a shadow cast on a vertical surface.

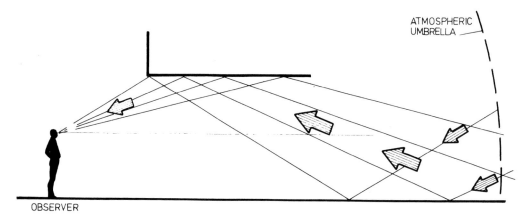

ATMOSPHERIC UMBRELLA

OBSERVER

66 An observer looking at the underside of an object.

The observer looking at the underside of a horizontal plane (**66**) will see this surface as a very efficient reflector of light rays from the atmospheric umbrella, which strike the horizontal ground plane at some distance behind the object, are reflected to its underside and then directed towards the observer's eye.

67 The underside is lighter than the vertical plane.

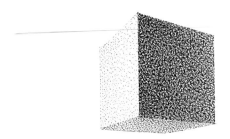

Because of its position, the underside is a more efficient reflector than the vertical plane seen in shade and will, therefore, appear slightly lighter (**67**).

68 Shadow on the vertical plane.

The shadow on the vertical surface will be slightly lighter in value than the shadow on the horizontal surface because it can reflect more light (**68**). The shadow on the vertical surface is usually in such a position that it reflects less light towards the observer's eye than does the vertical surface seen in shade, so it will be slightly darker in value.

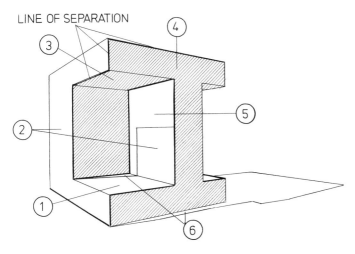

LINE OF SEPARATION

All of the conditions discussed so far have been applied in this drawing (**69**). The object is seen under conditions consistent with a light source located behind the observer and to his left. Shade areas are hatched and the line of separation is shown. (The line of separation is the line between planes seen in light and those seen in shade.) This careful identification of the line of separation is an extremely important step, which is often ignored by the inexperienced. Of equal importance is the identification of the light, shade and shadow areas, because each must be rendered using its correct value, so that the changes of direction of the planes will still be seen in the shade and shadow areas as they appear in reality.

In this diagram of values (the tonal pattern), each surface has been allocated a number from 1 to 6 to indicate the gradation from the lightest to the darkest value.

1 The horizontal surface seen in light is the lightest value.
2 The vertical surface seen in light.
3 The horizontal surface (underside) seen in shade.
4 The vertical surface seen in shade.
5 The vertical surface seen in shadow.
6 The horizontal surface seen in shadow is the darkest value on the rendering.

To avoid possible confusion it should be stressed that the numbers used for the value identification indicate only the order of darkness of the surfaces and do not indicate the values related to the value scale, which will be introduced later (see p. 69).

70 When all the surfaces have the same value the illusion of three dimensions is lost.

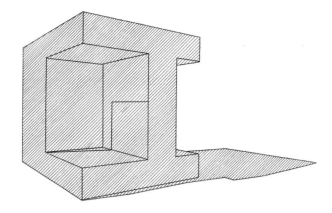

If the value pattern is ignored the illusion of a third dimension is lost, as in this illustration (70) where light, shade and shadow have been 'rendered' using one overall value.

71 A rendering without the addition of atmospherics.

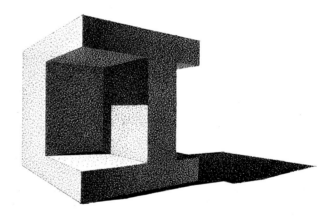

Though this is not the final rendering in this series, it shows a strong illusion of a third dimension and is easy to understand (71). It is reasonably successful, but lacks the important element of atmospheric effect on the dynamic surfaces. As the distance between the observer and the object or part of the object increases the image will become less clear and less sharply defined, because fewer light rays will make the journey through the atmosphere without being deflected from their original course.

The observer (72) is looking at the ground plane, a horizontal surface, receding into the distance until it disappears over the horizon. The part closest to him will be seen as the truest value of this horizontal surface and as it recedes from him his view will be interfered with by the atmospheric effect, so that he will no longer see it at its true value. If the surface goes far enough into the distance, it will be impossible for him to distinguish the horizontal plane at all, because it will become neutral, in common with everything else. Observation will confirm the neutralizing effect of atmospherics over great distances.

This neutralizing effect reduces all values, both light and dark, as well as all colours and textures to a neutral condition (73, overleaf). Because atmospherics cause this neutralizing, it starts immediately a surface begins to recede from an observer and under most normal circumstances proceeds at a constant rate, so that an even gradation of value will be seen as the surface recedes.

72 An observer looking at a horizontal surface.

73 Atmospheric effect reduces light and dark values as the distance from the observer increases. The result is reducing contrasts.

74 Three values receding.

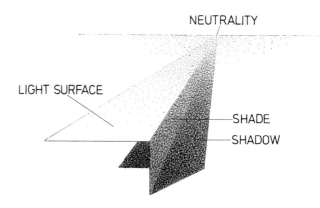

NEUTRALITY

LIGHT SURFACE

SHADE

SHADOW

The illustration (**74**) shows a horizontal plane in light, a vertical plane in shade and the shadow cast on the horizontal ground plane. Irrespective of what conditions cause the value on each plane, i.e. whether it is a light or dark surface or seen in shade or shadow, each value will begin to neutralize as it starts to recede from the observer and will continue to do so as far as the surface is seen. As the distance increases, the three elements in this illustration become harder to distinguish from one another and, if continued far enough, will disappear completely in the general neutrality which is associated with great distance.

75 Two groups of panels.

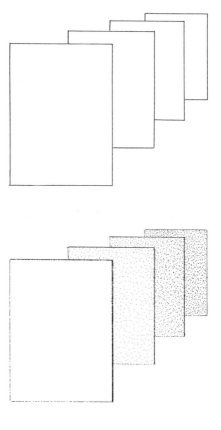

Rather than this neutralizing effect of atmospherics being a problem to the artist or illustrator, it is of enormous value because it allows for a dynamic surface to be rendered in a dynamic way, which can only add to the illusion of a third dimension in a pictorial representation.

This can be demonstrated by using four vertical planes placed at different distances from the observer (75). The top group of panels is shown without atmospheric effect and, when compared with the four identical panels below them, which have been rendered using atmospheric effect, the increased illusion of depth in the latter is obvious. (The atmospheric effect is slightly exaggerated in this simple explanatory diagram.) This should be no surprise because atmospheric effect is an optical fact of life and is present in everything that is seen, irrespective of the size of the object and whether or not the observer is trained to see the effect.

Admittedly, it is more difficult to demonstrate on some objects such as this small box (76), but a carefully taken and enlarged photograph of a very small object will show evidence of gradation in the values of the receding surfaces.

76 If the receding surfaces of this small box are carefully examined, gradations of value can be discerned.

77 A flat tone on a dynamic
surface and an incorrect
rendering.

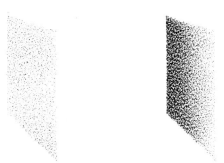

In this example (77), the dynamic plane on the left is rendered using a flat ungraduated tone and, because such conditions are contrary to optical laws, the result is flat and without a strong illusion of a third dimension.

The visual evidence presented to the observer by this drawing, or any other similar type of treatment lacking true atmospheric effect on a dynamic plane is contrary to what is seen when looking at the actual object. The lines of the object tell the observer that the plane is receding from him, but the flat tone of the plane tells him that it is not, because only a static plane will present an ungraduated tone. Which part of the visual evidence should the observer believe? If the artist or illustrator offers confused or contradictory information in drawn images, anyone looking at the picture will be confused as to exactly what message is really intended.

The dynamic plane on the right is rendered with gradation, but this image is just as confusing as the one on the left, because the gradation is reversed. Atmospheric effect causes a value to tend towards neutrality as its distance from the observer's eye increases; the truest value is seen closest to the observer's eye.

78 A dynamic plane whose
tone is graduated correctly.

When all of the requirements consistent with optical fact are satisfied, as in this illustration (78), there is no longer a contradiction of visual evidence, and anyone looking at the picture need no longer be confused as to exactly which conditions have been portrayed. Very simply, if these drawings have as their main purpose the creation of an illusion of a third dimension, the two illustrations in the preceding figure must be wrong and this one must be right. This conclusion is a matter of visual literacy being used in a graphic form to convey a literate pictorial representation; valid optical laws have been acknowledged and used.

When atmospheric effect is used on the dynamic surfaces of an object the drawing offers a substantially increased illusion of a third dimension (79). The rendering becomes easier to read because each surface, whether seen in light, shade or shadow, is easily related to those adjacent to it and the object as a whole. Note that even with atmospheric effect the tonal pattern is strictly maintained.

79 A cut cube with atmospherics.

80 An abstract design of a three-dimensional pattern based on spheres. The tone pattern is extremely useful to the artist or illustrator irrespective of the type of expression or medium chosen for a pictorial composition.

The tonal pattern is extremely useful to the artist or illustrator, no matter what type of expression or medium is chosen for pictorial communication. This pen-and-ink illustration (80) shows a three-dimensional composition using spheres as the theme. The location of the spheres, whether floating in front of the main pattern plane or taking a position in it, is controlled by a combination of light and shade and atmospheric effect. The illusion of the third dimension is achieved without the use of perspective in the usual sense, but is the result of the optical evidence by which the observer's eye establishes the location of surfaces in space and in relation to one another. This effect is carefully controlled and every surface has been rendered in relation to its neighbour and the design as a whole, so that the observer sees exactly what he is intended to see. A sound understanding of light and shade and atmospheric effect plus a good working knowledge of the elements and principles of design (composition) are the essentials for this type of rendering.

81 Giambattista Piranesi, *Carceri d'Invenzione*, engraving. The ability of surfaces to receive and reflect or absorb light is of major concern to the artist.

Light reflection and absorption

An aspect of reflected light which must be understood is the ability of various values to reflect or absorb light rays. This has already been mentioned in the list of properties of light rays and is an important element in understanding the rendering of the effects of light.

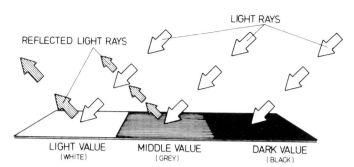

82 Light values reflect more light.

LIGHT RAYS

REFLECTED LIGHT RAYS

LIGHT VALUE
(WHITE)

MIDDLE VALUE
(GREY)

DARK VALUE
(BLACK)

Light values reflect more light rays than dark ones (82). When three different values are subjected to the same amount of light, the white surface reflects an amount of light equal to that striking it, the mid-grey one reflects only about half the amount of light striking it and the black surface reflects none. Something must happen to the light rays that are not reflected and, very simply, they are absorbed by the surface they strike.

83 The reflection and absorption of light rays by white and black surfaces.

WHITE SURFACE

WHITE ABSORBS NO LIGHT
RAYS AND REFLECTS ALL
OF THEM

BLACK SURFACE

BLACK ABSORBS ALL LIGHT
RAYS AND REFLECTS NONE

In theory, white absorbs no light rays and reflects all which strike it (83). In practice, the white found in everyday articles varies in whiteness and therefore it varies a little in its ability to absorb and reflect light rays. For the purpose here, white is considered to be true white, which absorbs no light rays and reflects all that strike it. White, the lightest value which can be obtained, is at one end of a scale of values which is laid out in equal steps of grey from white to black, the darkest value which can be obtained. Black, in theory, absorbs all light rays and reflects none, so logically it must be impossible to see it. In practice, the black used in everyday articles can be seen, so it cannot be true black. There are other factors contributing to this visibility of black, e.g. the type of surface, its texture, shape and the location of the light source. However, for the purposes of understanding the basic principles it is assumed that the black surface shown is true black.

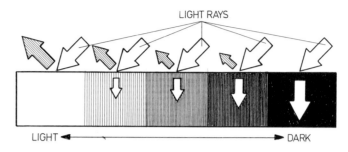

LIGHT RAYS

LIGHT ◄─────────────────────► DARK

The diagram (84) shows the increasing ability of a surface to absorb light rays at the expense of its ability to reflect them when black is added in increasing quantities. From these demonstrations it can be understood that darker surfaces are less efficient reflectors than lighter ones because they absorb more light rays. It naturally follows that as light rays strike a darker surface some of them are lost by absorption and the reflected light rays are not as numerous as the original light rays.

85 Diagram showing the reduction of light rays as they are reflected from two medium value surfaces.

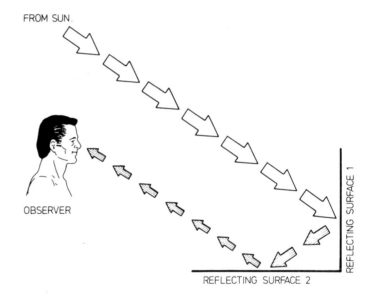

FROM SUN

OBSERVER

REFLECTING SURFACE 1

REFLECTING SURFACE 2

By following light rays as they are reflected from one surface to another and from there to the observer's eye (and the size of the arrows indicates the decreasing ability of each surface to reflect the light rays), the approximate value of each surface can be determined (85). The two surfaces shown must be mid-grey, because if they were white there would be virtually no reduction in the number of the original light rays finally reflected in the direction of the observer's eye. If the surfaces were black the light rays would be completely absorbed by the first 'reflecting' surface, no light would be reflected to the second surface or to the eye of the observer, who would not see the two surfaces. As previously stated, experience shows that in reality black objects and surfaces are seen, so what is known as black must be treated in rendering as a very dark grey, which is capable of reflecting enough light for it to be seen.

The importance of these principles may not be evident at first, but in many renderings where it is not always possible to work from direct observation, this knowledge of the amount of light being reflected to or from a surface could be essential.

Understanding the effects of the atmosphere and the principles of reflection and absorption enables the renderer to calculate exactly what will happen to a surface, no matter what the lighting conditions are or where the surface is placed in relation to the observer. If produced without this knowledge and the skill to apply it a rendering can, and usually will, lack the subtleties which are an important part of the works of the masters.

86 An understanding of the principles of absorption and reflection is extremely important when it is not possible to work from direct observation.

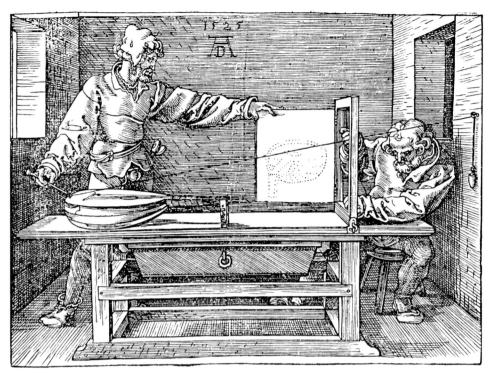

87 Albrecht Dürer, *Draughtsman Drawing a Lute*, woodcut, 1525. An accurate drawing based on the principles of perspective and the correct projection of shadows is essential to competent rendering.

The drawing

An accurate line drawing constructed in accordance with the principles of perspective and three-dimensional shadow projection is a basic essential for a competent rendering. However, if the final rendering is to satisfy the requirements of a specific idea or theme, certain decisions must be made concerning the station point in relation to the object before the drawing is started.

The illustration (**88**) is provided here for convenient, quick revision of basic two-point perspective construction. A full explanation can be found in *Basic Perspective*.

In the one-point perspective all edges of the cube are either at right angles to or parallel with the observer's centre line of vision. The vertical face of the cube is seen as a static plane and by itself gives no illusion of a third dimension. The elevation of the observer's eye enables him to see the top surface of the cube, which is a dynamic plane. The dynamic plane appears to recede from him and it is this rather than the static plane which introduces the suggestion of a third dimension (**89**).

From the foregoing, it can be seen that the static plane by itself does not produce the illusion of a third dimension because none of the elements of perspective is present. However, when a dynamic plane is introduced, provided it conforms to the optical laws, the illusion of a third dimension is produced. Therefore, it reasonably follows that an image made up of dynamic planes will give a stronger il-

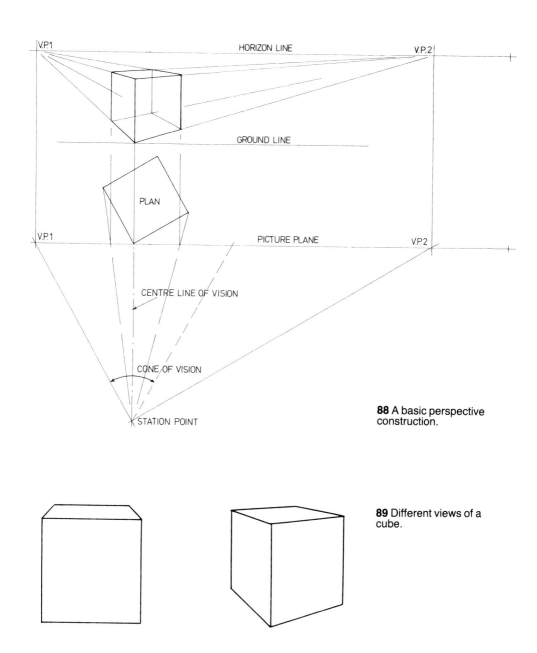

88 A basic perspective construction.

89 Different views of a cube.

lusion of a third dimension than an image composed of static planes.

The second example, a two-point perspective, shows the same cube as in the previous example but turned on its vertical axis until none of its sides is either at right angles to or parallel with the observer's centre line of vision. The observer will see the three surfaces of the cube as dynamic planes. Each surface offers evidence of the three basic optical laws and the result is a much stronger illusion of a third dimension than was apparent in the first example.

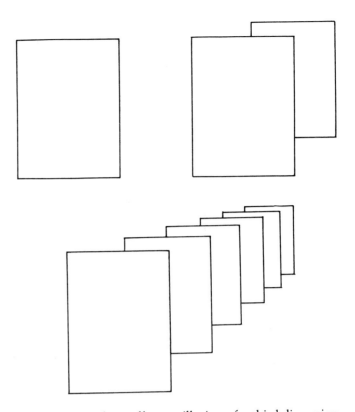

90 Static planes.

One static plane offers no illusion of a third dimension, but if a second static plane is added, provided it is carefully placed in accordance with the basic optical laws, there is an immediate introduction of the illusion of a third dimension (90). The conditions implied are that a second panel of the same size as the first one has been placed at some distance behind the front panel. The apparent overlapping of the back panel by the front one reinforces the illusion of the third dimension. From this evidence, it can be seen that much has been implied by the careful size control and the placing of the second panel. Though there is no way that the size of the second panel can be measured or the distance between the two established, there is a strong feeling that in reality the two panels are the same size. That the back one looks smaller than the front one is quite easily attributed to the result of basic optical laws consistent with perspective.

The illusion of a third dimension is further reinforced in the third part of this illustration, where more panels have been carefully introduced to give the impression that they are the same size and equal distances apart. Any doubts which might have been in the observer's mind have now been removed and the evidence is easily interpreted as a strong illusion of distance.

Examination of this illustration of a number of static panels placed behind one another shows that, though not drawn, the illusion of parallel lines converging at a constant rate as they recede from the observer is very strong.

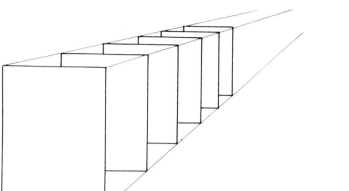

91 Static planes with receding lines drawn.

The basic optical law of convergence would appear to be well satisfied here (**91**), although the lines shown in this illustration were not drawn on it. Secondly, the size of the panels appears to be decreasing at a constant rate as the viewing distance increases, which means that the basic optical law of diminution is strongly implied. The distance between the panels appears to be decreasing at a constant rate as the viewing distance increases so the basic law of foreshortening is satisfied. The three basic optical laws of perspective have been satisfied in both drawings, so the illusion of a third dimension is quite strong. To this can be added what I call a minor optical law known as overlapping.

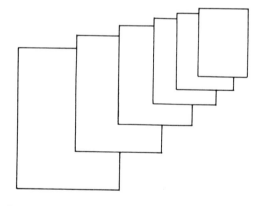

92 Overlapping planes of different sizes.

I call overlapping a minor optical law because it is successful only when it is in accord with the major optical laws. For example, if a number of static panels of varying sizes are placed so that they partially overlap one another as shown in this illustration (**92**), the result is somewhat confusing. One thing that is certain is that the illusion of a third dimension is not obvious. One might be persuaded that the drawing represents rectangles of various sizes which could have been cut out of paper and laid one on top of the other in order of size. Though overlapping has been used, the result is confusing for the observer, because this overlapping is not consistent with the major optical laws.

93 Multiple panels creating a third dimension.

A number of different components can be utilized to produce an illusion of a third dimension in a line drawing. For example, a vertical dynamic panel, if extended into the distance, will produce a convincing illusion of a third dimension (**93**). The same can be said of the horizontal dynamic panel. From this it should be obvious that if a line drawing is made up of dynamic planes surrounded by lines which conform to the basic optical laws, the foundations of the illusion of a third dimension can be effectively laid. However, this is only a foundation and whilst it can help to some degree to create the illusion of a third dimension, a line drawing of an object can seldom rival the illusion created when the same line drawing is correctly rendered.

No line drawing of an object or view which is to be the basis of a rendering can be considered complete unless the shadow shapes for the chosen light source have been correctly constructed on it.

Because it is known that light rays from the sun travel in straight parallel lines, vanishing points can be located in a perspective construction for the actual light rays and their plans, both of which are necessary for the shadow shape construction in perspective. Shown here (**94**) is the basic shadow construction for a cube where the light source (the sun) is behind the observer and to his left. In (**95**) the shadow shape has been completed. This process is explained fully in *Creative Perspective*.

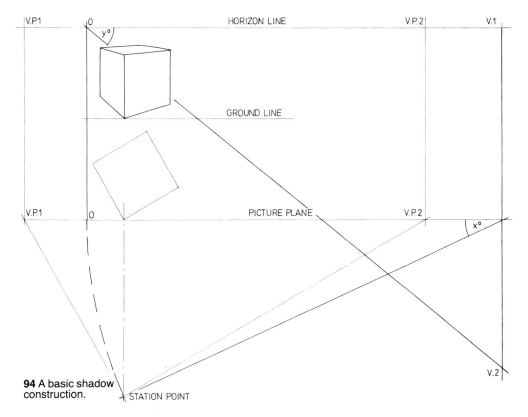

V.P.1   O   HORIZON LINE   V.P.2   V.1
        y°

GROUND LINE

V.P.1   O   PICTURE PLANE   V.P.2

x°

V.2

94 A basic shadow
construction.   STATION POINT

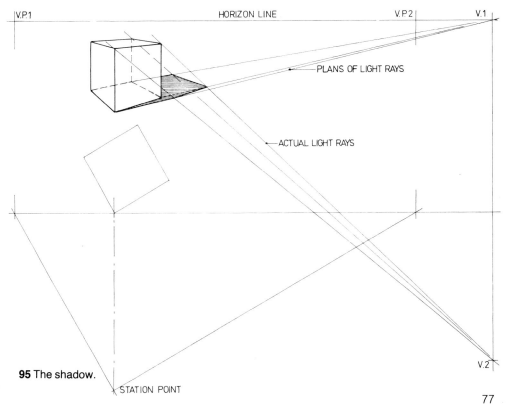

V.P.1   HORIZON LINE   V.P.2   V.1

PLANS OF LIGHT RAYS

ACTUAL LIGHT RAYS

V.2

95 The shadow.   STATION POINT

96 The line of separation.

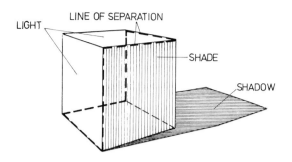

Once the shadow shape for an object, a cube in this example (**96**), has been constructed it is necessary to identify the line of separation on the object. As previously stated, the line of separation is the line on an object that separates the parts seen in light from those seen in shade. The line of separation on this cube seen under the conditions established in the preceding shadow construction divides it exactly in halves, so that three surfaces are in light and three are in shade. Examination will show that the outline of the shadow shape of an object is, in fact, the shadow of its line of separation. If for no other reason, this fact alone would make the identification of the line of separation on an object an essential step in the preparation of a drawing for rendering.

In rendering it is essential that shade and shadow are correctly identified, clearly distinguished and correctly rendered, so it is worth repeating their definitions: 'Shade exists when a surface is turned away from a light source' and 'Shadow exists when an opaque object is placed between a light source and a surface on which the light would normally fall.'

Students are advised to do all preparatory work as it becomes possible and to develop a logical system or sequence of work procedures for preparing a drawing for rendering. Such a logical system will save time and possibly costly errors when working in the commercial world.

Substantial tracing paper (115 gsm +) is recommended for all perspective constructions that are to form the basis for renderings. There are a number of very good reasons for this, not the least of which is that it is fairly inexpensive when compared with other papers. Other reasons will become obvious as the principles of rendering are developed.

When the perspective construction of the object is finished, with its shadow shapes completed and the line of separation identified, the drawing is ready to be transferred to the final sheet of paper, board or canvas for the rendering to be made in any medium or technique. Only the very inexperienced or the very unwise would even consider rendering a construction drawing with all of its structural lines, identifying marks, corrected mistakes and grubby marks.

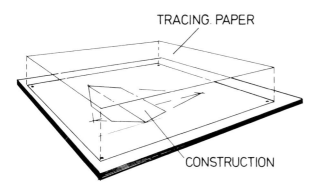

TRACING PAPER

CONSTRUCTION

97 The direct tracing method.

Depending on the requirements of the rendering, the process of transferring the construction drawing on to the final surface varies. For example, if tracing paper is to be used for the rendering, the final sheet can be laid over the construction sheet and fixed so that it cannot move (**97**). The final drawing can then be traced and the rendering developed over the original construction.

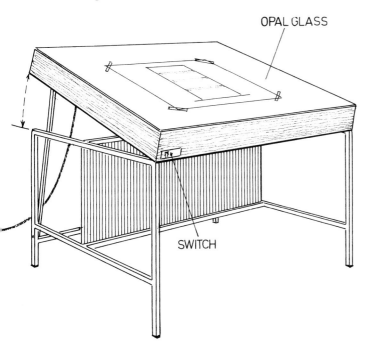

OPAL GLASS

SWITCH

98 A light table

If the final rendering is to be on one of the many drawing papers, a light table can be used for a process similar to that used for tracing paper. The original drawing is fixed to the light table and the drawing paper is fixed over it (**98**), so that the lines can be traced on to the final sheet.

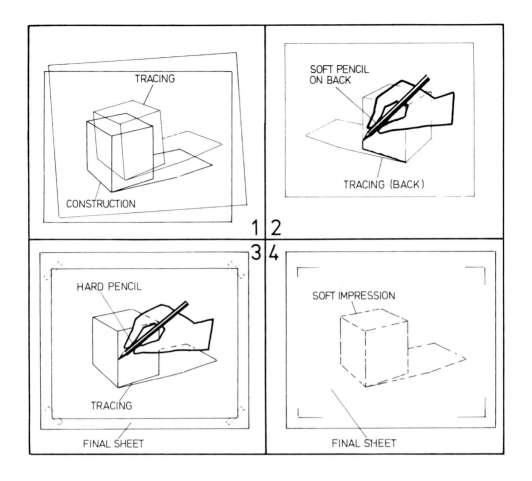

1 | 2
3 | 4

TRACING

CONSTRUCTION

SOFT PENCIL
ON BACK

TRACING (BACK)

HARD PENCIL

TRACING

FINAL SHEET

SOFT IMPRESSION

FINAL SHEET

99 The transfer method, drawing on the back of a sheet.

If a light table is not available, one very good simple method for transferring the construction drawing to the final sheet is to turn the construction sheet face downwards and, using a reasonably soft grade of pencil, such as HB, B, or 2B, draw over all of the relevant lines of the construction drawing (**99**). Place the construction drawing, face up, over the final sheet and fix it so that it cannot move. Using just enough pressure to obtain an imprint on the final sheet, carefully draw over the required lines so they are lightly transferred to the final sheet below. This method can also be used for transferring construction drawings to heavy card, fashion board, canvas or any other solid opaque material on which the final rendering might be made.

Once the drawing has been transferred to the final sheet it is possible to commence the rendering.

Whether pencil, pen, or brush is used, the pattern of light and shade, shadow, contrasts, textures and atmospheric effect will be the same. In other words, the means of expression may vary but the value pattern of an object or view will not, unless the conditions under which it is seen are changed.

100 Vincent Van Gogh, *Vagrant with Hat and Stick*, 1882. Van Gogh used beautifully controlled contrasts for this pencil drawing.

Contrast

The basic tonal pattern (shown here [101] in diagrammatic form with flat ungraded tones) demonstrates that constrast, or difference in tone, is responsible for much of the illusion of the change of direction of the surfaces.

101 The basic tonal pattern.

102 Maximum contrast is seen in the foreground; contrasts between light and dark surfaces are greater nearer to the observer and diminish as distance increases.

83

103 A rendering of a cube.

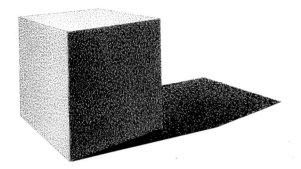

The introduction of atmospheric effect to the surfaces of the cube causes each tone to be slightly modified in value as the surfaces recede from the observer. This means that the closest part of a surface is seen at its truest value or colour and also that the area of greatest contrast will occur where these surfaces meet (**103, 104**).

This is consistent with atmospheric effect and basic optical laws. As each surface recedes from the observer's eye its value tends towards neutrality and the contrast between these surfaces will be reduced. Naturally, the further they recede into the distance the nearer to true neutrality they will become until ultimately all will become neutral and indistinguishable by the observer.

Because the surfaces of the cube in the illustration do not extend to great distances from the observer's eye the atmospheric effect on them must be fairly slight but, because all three are seen as dynamic planes, they cannot be rendered as flat tones. To do so would imply that they are static planes, which is a contradiction of all the other visual information in the drawing. The atmospheric effect must be clear enough to be seen, but it should not be so obvious that it dominates the rendering.

104 A diagram of true values.

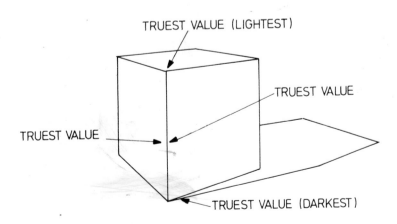

TRUEST VALUE (LIGHTEST)

TRUEST VALUE

TRUEST VALUE

TRUEST VALUE (DARKEST)

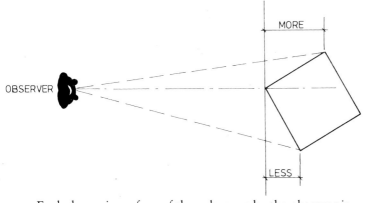

Each dynamic surface of the cube seen by the observer is at a different angle to his centre line of vision, so the three surfaces appear to recede at different rates. Because of this, each will have a slightly different amount of greying of the tone on its surface. Here (105) the distances are comparatively small and therefore the differences in the rate of greying will be very small. Though this point is only a minor one, it is made because many inexperienced renderers exaggerate the atmospheric effect so much that the furthest value seen on a surface in shade is often shown as a lighter value than the furthest value of a side seen in light. Under normal conditions, in a cube of the size shown here, this is impossible. If the atmospheric effect is understood it should be obvious that the neutralizing effect on any surface seen in light could never cause it to be seen as a value darker than that on a surface seen in shade, no matter what distance variations are involved.

106 Exaggerated atmospherics.

This rendering (106) of the cube seen from the position shown in the preceding illustration shows dramatically exaggerated value changes instead of the subtle, even ones that are consistent with basic optical laws. The exaggerated gradation implies enormous variations in distance from the observer's eye but the implied size of the cube is no more than a metre or so. A literate observer confronted with such conflicting evidence becomes confused and frustrated with the picture because it is not consistent with basic optical laws and, therefore, does not offer evidence that is consistent with reality. Because the rendering fails to communicate a clear picture of the cube in graphically literate terms it is unsuccessful.

107 A complete rendering of a cube and ground plane.

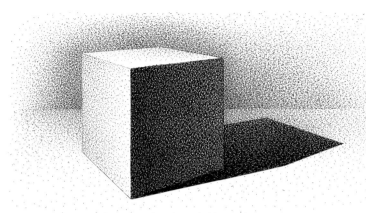

In the correct interpretation of the atmospheric effect on the cube, the maximum constrast on the drawing will be between the nearest part of the shadow cast by the object and the plane in light on which the shadow is cast (**107**).

Basic optical laws establish that constrasts decrease as distance from the observer's eye increases. To achieve this reduced contrast between the distant shadow and its adjacent lit area, the ground plane must be rendered with atmospheric effect to relate the cube to its base plane. In other words, atmospheric effect must be applied to everything within the picture area, not just some selected surfaces. Remember this, for it can often make the difference between good and bad renderings, even in simple ones such as those used to illustrate the basic principles in this book.

This rendering is completed with the introduction of a mid-value background plane to reduce the contrasts on the most distant parts of the cube and the background. The background in conjunction with the dynamic base plane helps greatly to increase the illusion of distance.

108 A rendering of a cut block and base plane.

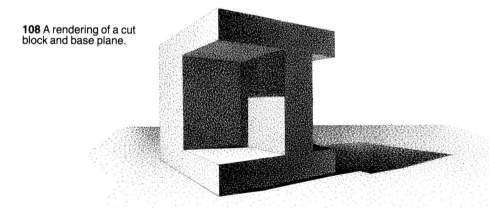

The addition here (**108**) of the rendered ground plane to the cut block first presented in (**69**) has introduced another dynamic plane, which helps the illusion of a third dimension. If the ground plane is not rendered with its atmospheric effect the observer is again faced with conflicting information. He 'knows' that the base on which the object is placed is a horizontal dynamic plane, but because it is offered in the rendering as a flat, even tone it seems to be a vertical static plane. This may appear pedantic, but the student of pictorial representation is reminded that, to be visually and graphically literate, it is necessary to present all of the evidence in a pictorial representation in accordance with basic optical laws. If this is not done confusion can and often does result.

109 Black on white, white on black.

110 Dark grey on light grey.

It is an observable fact, supported by research, that the eye is attracted by strong contrasts, e.g. black on white, white on black, black on yellow, red on white, white on red, green on white. The maximum contrast of black on white (**109**) is normally used for the printed text in books and newspapers because experience has shown that such a practice makes print easier to read.

If, for example, medium grey on a slightly lighter grey were used (**110**), the contrast would be greatly reduced, making it more difficult to differentiate between the letters and the background. The fact that different degrees of contrast have different impacts on the human eye has been known and used in art and graphics for many centuries.

111 A palaeolithic cave painting of a bison, in Lascaux in the Dordogne region of France. From the earliest times contrast has been used to draw attention to the most important part of a picture.

As Western art has developed from the palaeolithic era (**111**), so has the practice of drawing attention to the most important parts of a picture (the centre of interest) by creating maximum contrasts in those parts. Students are encouraged to examine Dürer's *The Four Horsemen of the Apocalypse* (**112**) and other masterpieces of Western art to confirm this fact for themselves. The observant student will see that other devices have also been used to draw attention to the important parts of the picture, but contrast is our main concern here. The competent artist knows that he must build maximum contrast at the centre of interest of his picture and that the other contrasts must be controlled so they do not compete with the main centre of interest.

The student is reminded of the basic principles of design or composition, though a full discussion of them is outside the scope of this book. These principles are: Proportion, Rhythm, Unity and Dominance, Balance, Harmony and Selection, Contrast.

Some authorities split unity and dominance, and harmony and selection into separate units but, whether the basic principles are considered as six or eight units, exactly the same basic ideas are expressed. In any valid design, whether two-dimensional or three-dimensional, these principles must be satisfied. Because of the importance of the basic principles of design (composition), students should study them in conjunction with their other studies in art, design or graphics so that all aspects of communicating with graphics are developed simultaneously. Everything should be used to contribute to the real purpose of the graphic representation, which is to communicate an image even if the image is that of an idea.

112 Albrecht Dürer, *The Four Horsemen of the Apocalypse*, woodcut, 1498. Dürer used contrast to draw attention to what he considered to be the most important parts of this woodcut.

113 Controlled contrasts can create the illusion of a third dimension, which can be subdued or exaggerated as required.

Contrasts created in accordance with basic optical laws can be used as compositional elements, but within the context of pictorial representation this is one of the most difficult and complex problems to be faced. Contrast is important because of its contribution to the location of objects or surfaces in relation to one another and to the picture area as a whole. By controlling contrasts, the relative importance of various elements and their distance from the observer can be established.

This illustration (**113**) relies almost entirely on the control of contrasts for its illusion of the third dimension. In accordance with the principles of design, the greatest contrasts are in the area of the centre of interest and they establish the location of the surfaces in this area in relation to the observer. All of the other surfaces, because of their various degrees of contrast, take up their positions relative to the surfaces established in the area of the centre of interest. Minimum use is made of conventional perspective and shadow construction with the major factor in creating a strong illusion of a third dimension being the control of contrasts.

From this example it can be seen how maximum contrasts could be used to establish the distance between the observer's eye and the object. At least this could be done if the maximum contrasts in the drawing were used on the closest object or part of an object and all others subordinated. In other words, by increasing the contrast in a rendering the distance between that increased contrast and the observer's eye will be effectively decreased.

Rendering cylinders, cones and spheres

114 Cylinders, cones and spheres.

The principle of contrasts decreasing as the distance between them and the observer's eye increases can be developed so that shapes other than cubes and rectangular prisms can be rendered. For example, cylinders, cones and spheres are made up of dynamic planes which need careful analysis before they can be rendered so that their shapes and forms are clearly expressed.

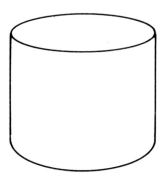

The cylinder, which is the simplest of this group of shapes, is made up of two parallel circular ends and a dynamic curved plane at right angles to the ends (**115**). If the cylinder is placed on one of its ends it is fairly simple to analyse its basic tonal pattern. As with any other shape to be rendered, a light source must first be located in relation to the object and the observer's chosen eye position. Because the light rays from the sun are parallel, one half of the cylinder will be in light and one half will be in shade.

116 The basic tonal pattern for a cylinder.

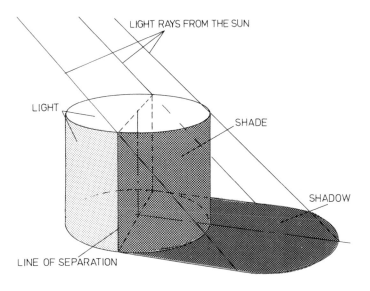

This illustration (**116**) shows how the light rays from the sun create the basic tonal pattern of the cylinder. The shadow cast by the cylinder on the base plane will start from the lower ends of the line of separation on the vertical surface. The value relationships of the surfaces of the cylinder are similar to those of the cube discussed earlier, but with one important difference: the vertical surface of the cylinder recedes from the observer at a constantly increasing rate, whereas the vertical surface of a cube recedes at a constant rate.

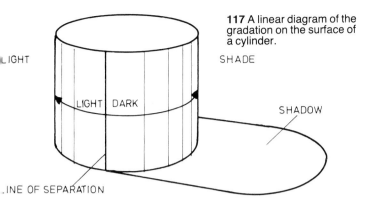

117 A linear diagram of the gradation on the surface of a cylinder.

LIGHT

SHADE

LIGHT | DARK

SHADOW

LINE OF SEPARATION

118 A tonal diagram showing gradation on the surface of a cylinder.

The gradation of the tone on the vertical surface of a cylinder will accelerate as the surface recedes from the observer, i.e. the greying process will increase at a faster rate than on the side of a cube (**117**).

In this cylinder, the truest value of the horizontal top surface will be at the front (**118**). As this surface recedes from the observer it will be affected by atmospherics and become slightly greyer. The nearest part of the vertical surface seen in light is adjacent to the line of separation and naturally its truest value will be seen in this area. Because of atmospheric effect and the increasing rate at which this surface recedes from the observer, the rate of greying of the value will be slightly increased as it moves round the curve of the surface.

That part of the vertical surface seen in shade nearest to the observer's eye is also near the line of separation. The line of separation is located on what can be described as the 'flattest' part of the curved surface that this observer sees, i.e. where the rate of atmospheric greying is at its slowest, so a much larger area of shade than light can be considered close to his eye. Because of this, the gradation caused by atmospheric effect will not commence at the line of separation as it did on the part of the surface seen in light. The darkest value will remain more or less constant over that small, 'flatter' part of the surface, but as its rate of receding from the observer's eye increases so the rate of greying will increase (**119**).

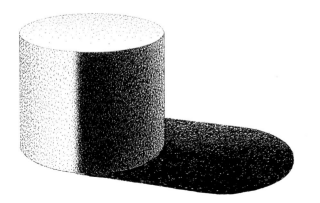

119 A rendering of the cylinder.

120 On a curved surface, there is a 'softening' effect of the line of separation instead of the 'hard', sharp line when surfaces abruptly change direction.

In this way the basic optical laws are satisfied and the information offered by the finished rendering is consistent with them. The shadow cast on the horizontal base plane will also be subject to atmospheric effect and will grey as the distance from the observer's eye increases.

Observation of reality shows that the line of separation on the surface of a cylinder is not a hard, sharp line between the light and shade as it is on a cube, where a sharp change of direction of planes is also involved. The line of separation on the vertical surface of a cylinder is a soft diffused line, which is expressed as an area of very rapid change from light to dark (120). This area of change is fairly small because the value change must be very dramatic if it is to present a convincing visual message (121).

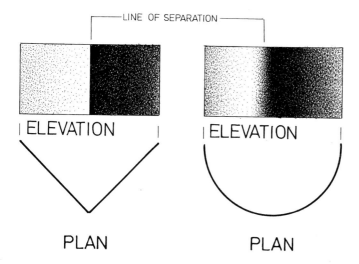

121 An explanation of the line of separation.

The rendering of the cylinder in (119) is the result of ideal conditions being used and it does not take into account any possible additional reflections which may result from other objects or surfaces, which may be located in positions that might affect what is seen. Nor does it take into account anything other than a smooth, light surface on the cylinder. Other types of surfaces would reflect light rays to the observer's eye in different ways resulting in different visual messages. Irrespective of the material of which the cylinder might be made, it is the renderer's prime responsibility to present an image of a cylindrical shape and then indicate a specific surface material and/or colour.

122 A group of four
cylinders of different
materials.

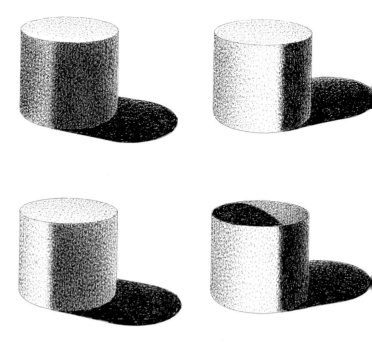

Four cylinders (one of them is hollow) of different materials and values are seen here (**122**) under different ideal conditions. Note that although the location of the observer and the light source may alter in relation to the cylinder, the tonal pattern and atmospheric effect remain valid. Irrespective of whether the cylinder is white or black the relationship of the surface tones remains the same. The darkest of all values will be seen in the shadow cast on the horizontal base plane.

An exception to the foregoing could be a white object on a white base plane (not illustrated). In that case the white base plane could cause an upset to the basic tonal pattern if the observer's eye were located where unusual reflections were allowed to interfere with the ideal conditions used to create the basic tonal pattern. Obviously, the use of a darker value base plane for a white object would tend to darken the shade and shadow areas whereas a white base plane would tend to lighten them. Another variation could occur when a black object is placed on a white base plane. Then it would be most likely that the shadow cast by the object on that base plane would appear lighter than the shade area on the vertical surface.

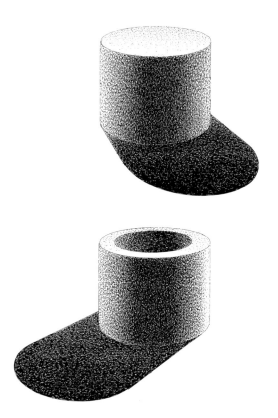

The student is warned that the modification or upset of the basic tonal pattern by the introduction of special conditions does not destroy its validity. In (**123**) the observer is located so that he sees no vertical surfaces in light. Obviously it is possible to change the basic tonal pattern of these cylinders or any other object by controlling the reflection of light rays. In some cases this is necessary but it is not something which should be attempted by the inexperienced. In practice the basic tonal pattern is not an absolute, nor is it something which must be rigidly adhered to at all times irrespective of special sets of conditions. It is exactly what it is claimed to be, a basis for the portrayal of form. Once the basic tonal pattern is mastered, students can experiment with it and develop it to their own special requirements. If this is done within the confines of basic optical laws and the reasons for any variation are clearly expressed in the pictorial representation, the result should be successful.

124 A rendering of a glass cylinder.

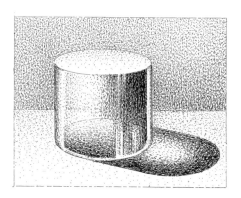

Portraying a cylinder made of a transparent material creates a new set of problems for the renderer. If the cylinder is made of glass, only two visual elements, transparency and reflected light, are available to the renderer (**124**). There will be no shade area on the cylinder because there are no opaque surfaces to be turned away from the light source, and the shadow will be different from that cast by opaque objects because light will be able to travel through the object with varying degrees of efficiency depending on the angle at which the light rays strike the glass surfaces. For the renderer to take advantage of the special characteristics of glass he must take great care when deciding the conditions under which the cylinder is to be viewed.

One method that is effective in the portrayal of glass is found in photography. Many experienced photographers often use a matt black base and background with carefully controlled lighting conditions to display the glass to the camera lens (**126**). In this way, advantage is taken of the varying degrees of transparency and the rather dramatic light reflections observed when looking at a glass object from a fixed eye position.

In one example in (**125**) a glass cylinder has been set up in the same way as that described for the photograph of a glass object. The illusion of glass is very strong, as might be expected when ideal conditions have been used for the rendering.

125 A glass cylinder shown on a light and a dark base.

126 The effects of reflection and transparency are more dramatic when glass is placed against a black background.

When a light tone is used as a base plane and background the problems of rendering glass are increased. Whilst reflected light is still important, its importance is reduced and transparency or the lack of it becomes the main element of the visual message. The whole expression under these conditions becomes more difficult because of the almost complete lack of really strong light and dark contrasts of the type seen in the first example. Once these strong contrasts are denied to the renderer, the problems of producing a satisfactory rendering are greatly increased and work must be carried out in a very subtle manner to achieve a valid result. The illustration shows a cylinder rendered under the conditions described, and though it lacks the dramatic impact of the one placed against the black background it still presents a satisfactory picture of glass.

127 This detail (right) from Hans Holbein the Younger's 1532 portrait of Georg Gisze (above) shows his masterly rendering of a glass vase.

The ability to draw glass or any other material or texture is very much dependent on knowing what to draw. The physical drawing skills, though important, do not necessarily play a decisive role in the process, but by the time most students have acquired the knowledge of what to draw they have also acquired sufficient skill to express that knowledge pictorially.

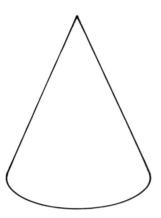

128 A line drawing of a cone.

The cone is a slightly more complex subject than the cylinder inasmuch as its curved surface slopes instead of being at right angles to its end (**128**). In many ways the rendering of a cone is similar to that of a cylinder, particularly with regard to the surfaces seen in light and shade and the line of separation.

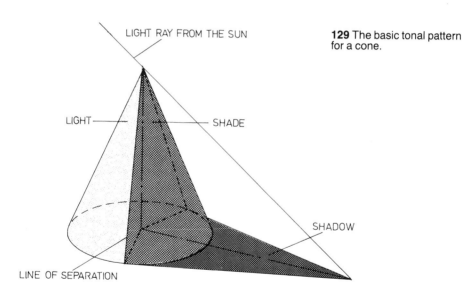

LIGHT RAY FROM THE SUN

LIGHT — SHADE

SHADOW

LINE OF SEPARATION

129 The basic tonal pattern for a cone.

A simple analysis of the light and shade, and shadow areas shows that each behaves similarly to those of the cylinder, except that the light and shade surfaces are sloping instead of vertical and the cone has no horizontal surface in light.

The diagram (**129**) shows how the light rays from the sun create the basic tonal pattern of the cone. As with the cylinder, the shadow cast by the cone will start from the bottom of the line of separation on the sloping curved surface.

130 Plan of a cone and its shadow.

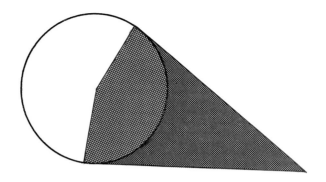

One point to note is that the line of separation of a cone does not meet the ends of a diameter of the base as it does on the cylinder. The light rays can travel further round the cone's sloping surface than round a vertical one and this results in a greater area of the surface being seen in light than in shade. The plan (130) shows the line of separation of the cone and the shadow cast on a horizontal base plane.

131 A linear diagram of the gradation on the surface of a cone.

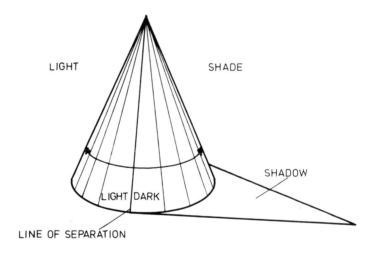

LIGHT   SHADE

SHADOW

LIGHT DARK

LINE OF SEPARATION

The atmospheric effect causes a gradation of the tones of the light and shade areas and it is important to note that each follows the tapering of the curved surface to the apex of the cone (131, 132). Any horizontal section through the cone will be circular in shape. Because of this, the round shape of the curved surface of the cone must be expressed to the very apex of the cone by rendering the gradation of the light and shade tones over the entire height of the cone. It is this condition which makes the cone a little more difficult to render than the cylinder.

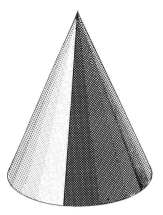

132 A tonal diagram showing gradation on the surface of a cone.

The rendering of the cone follows very closely the pattern for the cylinder (**133**). The truest value of the light, shade and shadow areas will be seen in the areas nearest to the observer's eye and as these areas recede their values will tend to neutralize. The line of separation will again be a diffused area of very quick value change from dark to light rather than a sharp line.

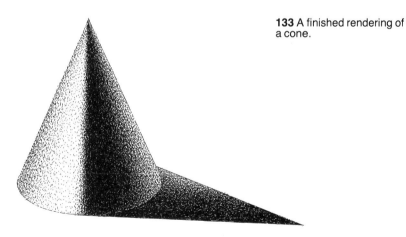

133 A finished rendering of a cone.

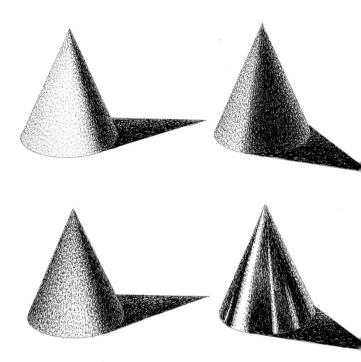

This illustration (**134**) shows a number of cones of different materials and values seen under different conditions. Though the location of the observer's eye and the light source might alter in relation to the cone, the tonal pattern remains valid as does the atmospheric effect.

135 Renderings of transparent cones against white and black backgrounds.

When considering transparent cones such as those made of glass or similar materials, the conditions already described for the glass cylinder still apply. The only special point to note is that the shadow becomes a very important clue to the material of which the cone is made. The light rays will travel more easily through that part of the cone which they strike more directly than those parts of the surface which form acute angles to the direction of the light rays. As a result, the shadow cast by the cone will have a darker outer edge which gradually becomes lighter towards the middle (135). This phenomenon can be seen when a drinking glass is placed in sunlight.

Light rays can travel through a glass surface more easily than they can pass through its edges (136). Simple experiment will show that it is easier to see through glass when the observer's centre line of vision is at or near a right angle to the surface of the glass than when his centre line of vision forms an angle of say five or ten degrees to the surface of the glass.

136 The light patch in the shadow of this drinking glass demonstrates that light is passing more easily through the central surface area of the glass than through the sides.

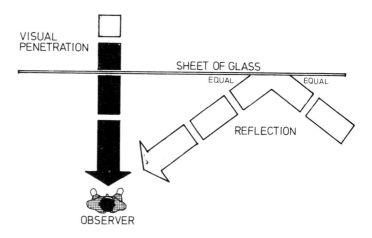

137 A sheet of glass and an observer.

VISUAL PENETRATION

SHEET OF GLASS

EQUAL   EQUAL

REFLECTION

OBSERVER

This principle is valid not only for cones and cylinders but for all glass objects. In fact, it can be said that rendering glass is fairly easy if the transparency and reflecting ability of a glass surface are understood and care is used in placing the object.

Because the surface of a sheet of glass is highly reflective, it will reflect light from the atmospheric umbrella in the direction of the observer's eye and thereby reduce his ability to penetrate visually the sheet of glass (**137**). Therefore, if that part of the rendering seen through the glass is reduced in contrast and value in comparison with the area seen without the glass, the result will be a convincing illusion of a sheet of glass (**138**). In a sense, only the edges of the sheet of glass have been drawn and the rest of the illusion is created by rendering the image of what is seen through it and the reflection on its surface. More simply, the rendering of glass is not so much a matter of being able to draw or render the material itself as of correctly interpreting its ability to reflect light and what is seen through it.

138 A sheet of glass in a rendering.

Rendering glass objects becomes a fairly simple process if it is remembered that the basis of a good pictorial representation is the ability to draw and render what is known together with what is seen. In this way advantage can be taken of the knowledge of ideal or near ideal conditions even when the object is not seen under these conditions.

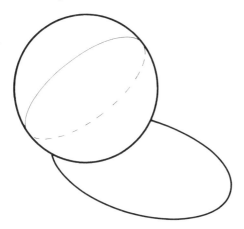

139 A line drawing of a sphere and its shadow.

The most difficult of all shapes to render is a sphere because it is one complex, dynamic surface. The surface recedes in all directions from the observer, so the entire surface must be rendered with gradation of values to communicate its roundness equally in its light and shade areas.

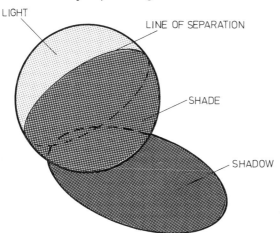

LIGHT

LINE OF SEPARATION

SHADE

SHADOW

140 The basic tonal pattern of a sphere.

In the basic tonal pattern of this sphere (**140**) the line of separation and the shadow indicate that the light source is to the left and behind the object. Because the light rays from the sun are parallel, the line of separation must be at right angles to them and will divide the sphere exactly in halves. (This is explained fully in *Creative Perspective*.) With the light source established, it is possible to locate the area seen in light and that seen in shade and then the parts in light and shade which are nearest to the observer's eye.

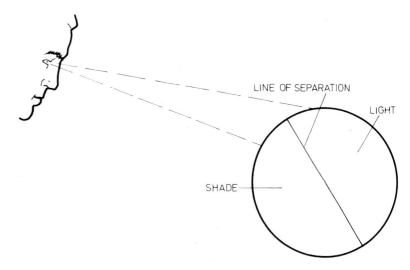

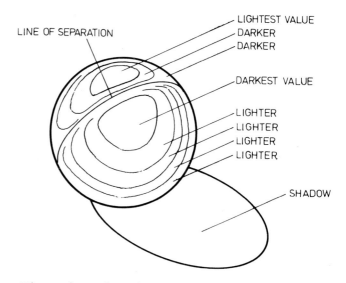

141 A diagram of an observer looking at a sphere (side elevation).

Because the observer's eye level is above the sphere (**141**), the areas in light and shade which are closest to the observer's eye will be towards the top of the sphere rather than in the middle.

142 The contour 'map' of a sphere.

The surface of a sphere is completely dynamic, i.e. it recedes in all directions from the observer's eye, so a diagram of its 'average contours' can be useful as a guide to the gradations of the surface tones (**142**).

The lightest area on the sphere will be that part seen in light nearest to the observer's eye and the darkest area will be the part seen in shade nearest to the observer's eye. As the surfaces seen in light and in shade recede from the observer's eye, both will be subject to atmospheric effect and will gradually become greyer. This greying effect will accelerate slightly as it nears the outer part of the sphere, because there the surface is receding at an increasing rate.

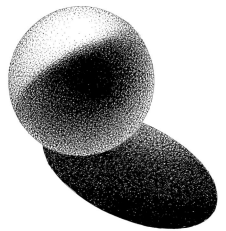

143 A finished rendering of a sphere.

The line of separation on a sphere is in reality a soft diffused line which is rendered as an area of very quick change from light to dark. However, in the rapidly receding outer area of the sphere seen by the observer the line of separation becomes almost impossible to identify. The shadow cast by the sphere will be the darkest value on the drawing. This rendering (**143**) shows how the darker shadow in conjunction with the gradation on the surface of the sphere increases the illusion of a third dimension and roundness on the sphere. One danger when drawing and rendering spheres is allowing the original contour lines to remain as value changes on the surface. Remember that these contour lines are only guides for rendering and the finished surface must appear smooth and without any sudden changes of value. Another point worth mentioning is that the lightest part of the surface of a sphere seen in light should not be a white spot with hard edges, because such a spot will create the illusion of a hole rather than a light part of the surface. Every part of the surface should be rendered as a dynamic plane, for any area which does not have gradation of value will tend to spoil the smooth roundness of the surface and the illusion of the sphere.

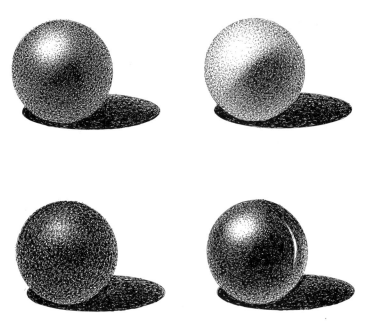

144 A group of four spheres of different materials.

Each of these four spheres (**144**) is of a different material or value but seen under the same lighting conditions. In each case the first concern of the renderer must be to indicate the spherical shape, because without this there is little point in attempting to express a specific material; the basic shape of the object must be evident before another aspect can be successfully introduced. This is very much the case when attempting to render glass spheres.

145 A rendering of two glass spheres, on light and dark backgrounds.

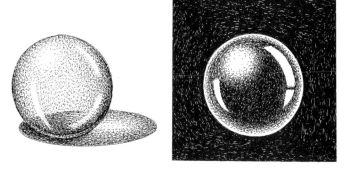

Dark and light bases and backgrounds have been used in these illustrations (**145**) and, as may be expected, the example with the dark base and background has the more dramatic impact and the more convincing illusion of glass. It is also the easier of the two renderings to produce. However, both examples are convincing renderings of glass spheres because both exploit the optical principles in the creation of the visual message, which is consistent with reality.

146 A rendering of a chrome sphere.

A chrome sphere offers the renderer another set of conditions (**146**). Though it is an opaque solid its reflecting surface is much more efficient than that of the transparent glass sphere. The surface of a chrome sphere is an almost perfect reflector which will reflect everything within its reflective range including the base on which it is placed, its own shadow, the observer, the light source and the atmospheric umbrella all round it. Light striking it will be reflected with virtually no reduction in strength. Because of this, the observer will see detailed images reflected by the surface facing in the general direction of his eye. He will see strong contrasts and even the smallest change of values on the surface of any reflected object. Observation of reality will confirm that no line of separation is visible on its surface, but it is essential for the renderer to locate it in the perspective construction because he will need it to be able to construct the shadow cast by the sphere.

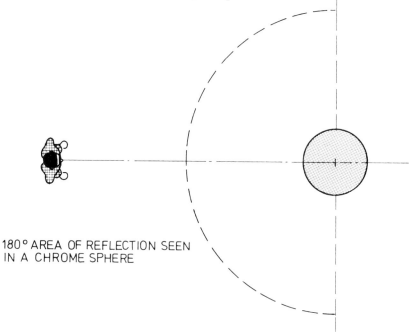

180° AREA OF REFLECTION SEEN IN A CHROME SPHERE

147 A chrome sphere reflects an area of 180 degrees.

The surface of the chrome sphere seen by the observer reflects an area of approximately 180 degrees both horizontally and vertically, at right angles to his centre line of vision (**147**). Therefore, an object reflected by the surface will be seen by the observer as a considerably condensed image following the curve of the surface of the sphere. The image he sees of himself, being on that part of the sphere nearest to him, will have far less distortion and will appear less condensed. Everything in front of that circumference of the sphere which represents its full extent seen by the observer will be reflected on the half of the sphere at which he is looking.

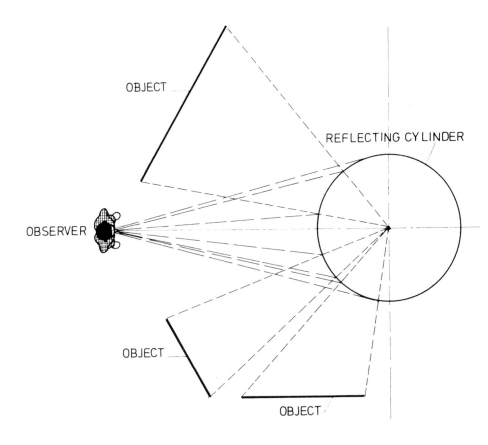

OBJECT

REFLECTING CYLINDER

OBSERVER

OBJECT

OBJECT

148 A simple explanation of reflections.

If the character of the distortions seen in the reflections of a highly reflective sphere is understood in general terms it is possible to construct images from the imagination or of objects which have yet to be built or manufactured. This is a distinct advantage to the designer, sculptor or artist.

Students are advised to explore further this aspect of reflection because a great deal can be learned from informed observation. Carefully taken photographs can also be of enormous assistance in this as well as other areas and a reference file of photographs of various objects, materials and textures under different lighting conditions will be indispensable to the serious student.

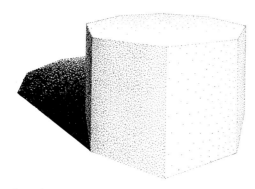

A multi-sided object such as an octagon (**149**) has much in common with cylinders and cones, except that the multi-sided object has positive changes of direction between planes. The tonal values of the various planes of the octagon are determined by the location of the source of the light rays.

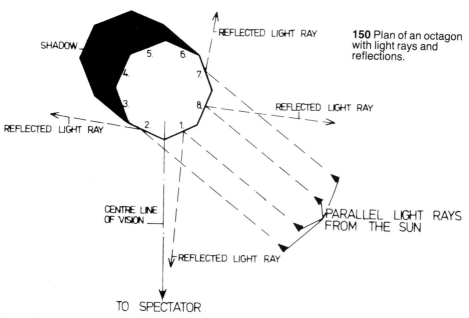

150 Plan of an octagon with light rays and reflections.

As with other objects, the top horizontal plane will be the lightest value and the plane seen in shade will be the darkest value on the surface of the object; the shadow cast on the horizontal ground plane will be the darkest value of all. The octagon shown has three vertical planes in three different directions seen in light, and one in shade which is in another direction. The three vertical surfaces seen in light will appear as three different values because, as the plan diagram shows (**150**), the angle of incidence and reflection of the light rays is different for each of these planes. Plane 1 will reflect more light rays in the direction of the observer's eye than will any of the other vertical planes and so will have the lightest value of the vertical planes.

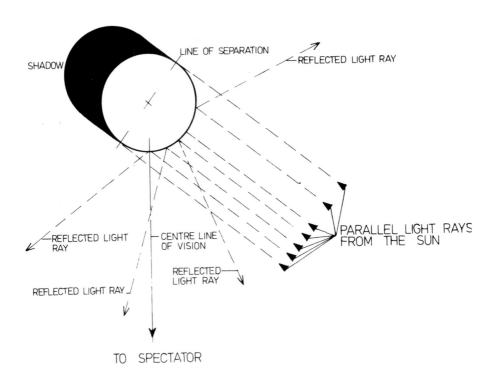

SHADOW

LINE OF SEPARATION

REFLECTED LIGHT RAY

REFLECTED LIGHT RAY

CENTRE LINE OF VISION

PARALLEL LIGHT RAYS FROM THE SUN

REFLECTED LIGHT RAY

REFLECTED LIGHT RAY

TO SPECTATOR

151 Plan of a cylinder with light rays and reflections.

When this principle of the reflection of light rays is applied to curved surfaces, such as those of a cylinder, it reinforces the results obtained using only the principles of atmospheric effect. This diagram (**151**) shows that the only light rays reflected back from the curved surface of the cylinder towards the observer are those from the areas seen in light, and the most efficient reflection is from that part of the surface nearest the observer. This basic principle of light reflection can be developed and used to produce more effective renderings.

152 A cube with three surfaces seen in light.

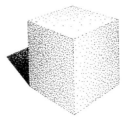

An important area of rendering where an understanding of reflected light rays is essential for a correct tonal interpretation is where all of the surfaces seen by the observer are in light. For example, the cube in the above illustration (**152**) is located so that light strikes all three surfaces seen by the observer.

The direction of the light rays is such that the horizontal top surface will be the lightest value, the vertical surface on the right will be slightly darker and the other vertical surface, because it tends to reflect light rays away from the observer, will be the darkest value of the three surfaces seen by the observer.

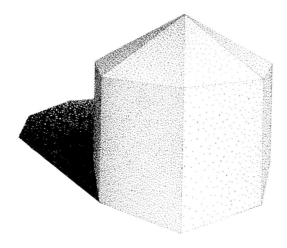

153 A rendering of an object with sloping surfaces.

Sloping surfaces add a further need for refinement of the tonal relationships of the surfaces of objects. Logically, a sloping surface must be a value somewhere between that on a horizontal surface and that on a vertical surface when all three are seen together in light or in shade. The value on a sloping surface is directly related to its angle of inclination, so that when it is almost horizontal its value will be fairly light. As one end is progressively raised to bring the surface closer to a vertical position its value will become progressively darker. This illustration (**153**) shows that when the sloping surfaces are related tonally to the vertical surfaces a strong illusion of a third dimension can be achieved.

Light rays are reflected, at least to some degree, by almost every surface they strike and even shade and shadow can be affected by reflected light. Light reflected from other surfaces on to objects that form the subject or part of the subject of a rendering needs to be considered very carefully. In the majority of cases its effects should be modified rather than exaggerated because they can upset the tonal pattern of an object and unnecessarily present the renderer with additional problems.

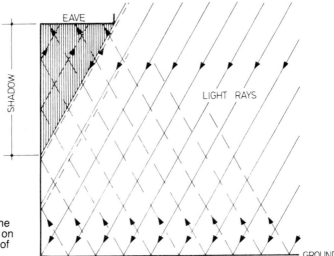

EAVE

SHADOW

LIGHT RAYS

GROUND

154 An explanation of the effects of reflected light on the overhanging eaves of buildings.

In spite of the danger from extraneous reflected light and the warning to use extreme care when dealing with it, there are instances where it can be used to advantage. An example of reflected light upsetting shade and shadow to advantage can be seen under the overhanging eaves of buildings (**154**). Because of its location, the underside of the overhang would be expected to be darker in value than the shadow it casts on the wall, but observation shows that such is not the case. The shadow cast on the wall is a darker value than the shade on the underside of the overhang. The reason for this reversal of the expected tonal relationship is explained in the diagram, which shows that light rays are reflected from the ground plane to the wall plane, including the part in shadow, but from both the ground plane and the wall plane to the underside of the eave overhang. It is the underside of the eave overhang, not the part of the wall in shadow, which receives more reflected light rays to reflect back in the direction of the observer. This causes the underside of the eave to be the lighter value. The light rays relected from the eave overhang back towards the observer are not shown, but

155 A sculptured block.

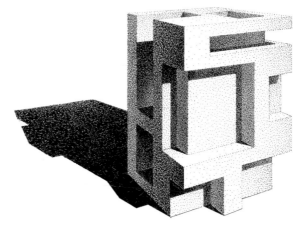

their direction should be understood easily. This effect can be best demonstrated with an example which depends to some degree on the interpretation of reflected light to produce a convincing rendering.

The sculptured block (155) shows how a consistent source of reflected light from the left has been used to lighten the shade areas which, in turn, intensify the illusion of a change of direction between surfaces seen in shade and those seen in shadow. Without this difference in value, much of the illusion of a convincing third dimension and some of the details of the shape of the object would be lost, to the detriment of the finished rendering.

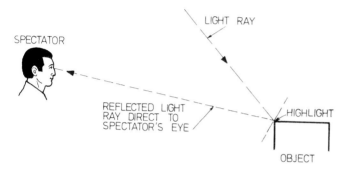

156 A diagram showing the path of a light ray and its reflection which is responsible for a highlight.

The final aspect of reflected light to be dealt with here is the much misunderstood phenomenon known as the highlight (156). The highlight is common on objects with reflective surfaces but is very seldom seen as clearly on objects that have matt surfaces. The diagram shows how light rays can strike a tiny area on an object's edge, which will very efficiently reflect them directly back to the observer's eye. The highlight seen by the observer would be a line of intensely light value at the intersection of the vertical and horizontal surfaces. Observation is the best source of information and if highlights are applied with understanding and extreme care they can be of considerable value in a rendering. However, they can be unfortunate distractions if they are not properly understood and used.

157 A cylinder with simple highlights shown.

Whilst the example in this illustration is a simple one (157), it shows that one highlight can occur on a vertical curved reflective surface and another, the very strong highlight, at the intersection of the vertical and the horizontal surfaces.

117

Rendering glass

With a general understanding of these aspects of rendering it is possible to extend one's knowledge by studying specific materials and textures. Glass is usually a transparent material with highly reflective surfaces which can be coloured or colourless and it can have various surface treatments, e.g. smooth, ribbed or textured. The first use of glass to be discussed here is for windows, where it is usually smooth surfaced, transparent and colourless. Because glass has two smooth surfaces which are highly reflective, rendering it is

not so much a problem of dealing with glass as a material in itself, but rather of dealing with the effect of things seen through it and/or reflected on its surfaces.

Observation shows that windows present a wide variety of effects when seen from outdoors. Some look light, some look dark, some are easily seen through and some reflect with almost mirror-like efficiency. Some are a mixture of reflections and visual penetration, while others are combinations of all or some of these aspects. This may seem very complex, but any confusion can be eliminated if the basic principles are understood.

158 When seen from the exterior, the appearance of windows depends on the viewing position with regard to visual penetration and/or reflection.

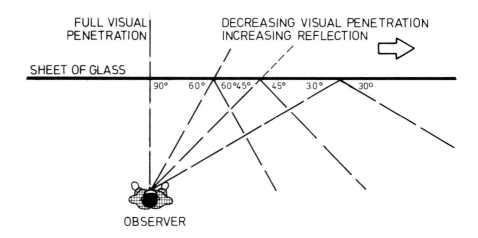

FULL VISUAL PENETRATION

DECREASING VISUAL PENETRATION
INCREASING REFLECTION

SHEET OF GLASS

90°   60°   60° 45°   45°   30°   30°

OBSERVER

159 Plan of an observer looking at a sheet of glass.

For example, when the observer's centre line of vision is at or near right angles to the surface of the glass he has the best chance of complete visual penetration (**159**). As the angle between the centre line of vision and the surface of the glass decreases, visual penetration also decreases and the reflecting ability of the glass surface increases. Simple experiment will show that a very small angle will result in mirror-like reflections.

160 As the angle between the centre line of vision and the glass surface is decreased, visual penetration is reduced.

As with practically every aspect of graphic communications, the lighting conditions are of prime importance to what is seen when looking at glass in windows. Under different lighting conditions windows will provide the observer with a variety of different visual messages.

Perhaps the simplest conditions to portray when rendering glass are when the observer is looking from outside into a well-lit room at night (**161**). Under these conditions the glass in the window will be completely transparent, so the glass in the window is inferred rather than actually rendered. Because the glass would normally be expected to be between the observer and the interior of the room and there is no logical reason for the glass not to be in its normal position its presence is automatically accepted.

Similar reasoning applies when the observer is located inside a room looking out of a window (**162**). Again, the glass is completely transparent and is accepted by inference rather than by illustration.

161 Looking into an artificially illuminated room at night.

162 Looking out through a window.

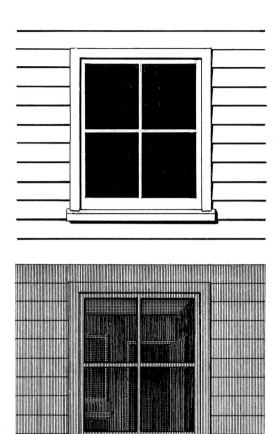

Unless affected by reflections, a window will look darker than the wall in which it is situated, even if the wall is in shade or shadow. Windows in walls which are seen in shade or shadow allow greater visual penetration than those in walls seen in full sunlight (**163**). A wall in sunlight reflects more light rays than one in shade or shadow, so that the contrast between the sunlit wall and the window will be very great and the window will appear to be almost black. This is probably the most commonly seen condition, especially in areas where the majority of buildings are of a domestic scale. The reason for this very dark appearance of the window area is that the interior of the room behind the window is much darker than the outside wall seen in sunlight. Under these conditions the iris of the eye adjusts to a smaller aperture to accommodate the brightly lit area and thereby reduces its ability to see into the darkened interior.

If the window is seen when the wall is in shade or shadow the exterior and interior lighting conditions are much closer to each other, contrast is greatly reduced and it is easier to penetrate visually the room behind the window. A window seen in shade or shadow will be slightly darker than the wall but the difference is not nearly as dramatic as when the wall is in sunlight.

It should be pointed out that the basic principles illustrated and discussed here are not intended as an inflexible set of rules for rendering all windows under all conditions. They are a starting point which, if combined with informed observation, should enable windows under any realistic conditions to be rendered in a believable way.

Two special sets of conditions are now worth examining (**164**). The first is where a shadow falls on part of a window the rest of which is in sunlight. The shadow on the glass will allow greater visual penetration of that area, which will therefore appear as a slightly lighter value than the area in sunlight.

The second of these special conditions is the window fitted with curtains or drapes. Because the window is seen in full sunlight the shadows of the window members play an important role in this rendering. The curtains or drapes are treated as any other opaque surface seen in sunlight and in all other aspects this rendering follows the principles discussed previously.

165 A diagram showing the transition from visual penetration of lower-level windows to full sky reflection in the upper windows of a multistorey building.

As previously stated, the two main characteristics of glass in buildings are its transparency and its reflective capacity. The effects of these characteristics are largely dependent on the location of the light source in relation to the glass and the observer and are very important when viewing a large multistorey building (**165**). For example, an observer looking up at the windows of a multistorey building will see the sky reflected in the upper windows and, under normal conditions, will be able to see through the glass into the lower floors where visual penetration will be even easier if the interior is artificially lit.

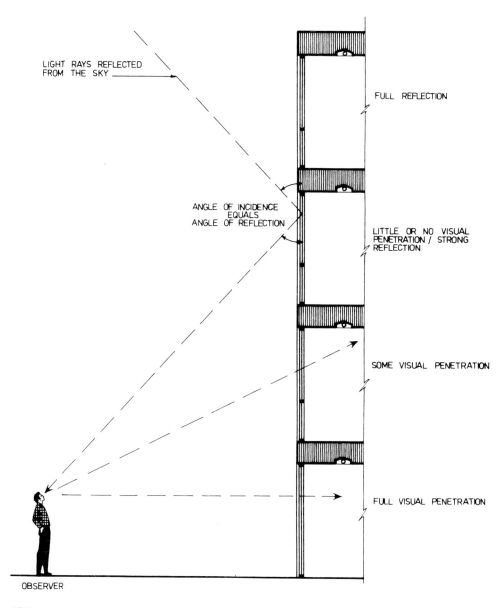

LIGHT RAYS REFLECTED FROM THE SKY

FULL REFLECTION

ANGLE OF INCIDENCE EQUALS ANGLE OF REFLECTION

LITTLE OR NO VISUAL PENETRATION / STRONG REFLECTION

SOME VISUAL PENETRATION

FULL VISUAL PENETRATION

OBSERVER

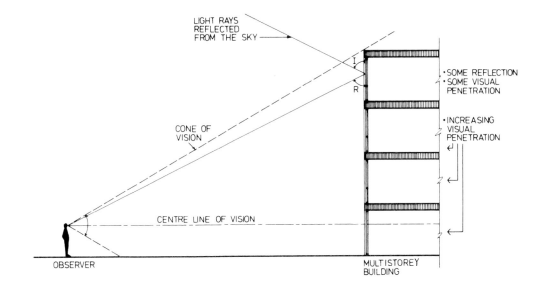

LIGHT RAYS
REFLECTED
FROM THE SKY

I

R

•SOME REFLECTION
•SOME VISUAL
 PENETRATION

•INCREASING
 VISUAL
 PENETRATION

CONE OF
VISION

CENTRE LINE OF VISION

OBSERVER

MULTISTOREY
BUILDING

Evidence confirming the principles illustrated in the diagram is much more easily seen in very tall buildings than in a building of the height shown. Nevertheless, this observer would see in the upper windows of this building a strong sky reflection which would gradually disappear as he moved further back from the building. Of course a rendering would never be attempted from such a close station point unless only a detail was required.

To set up a perspective view of the whole building, the distance between the building and the observer would have to be increased until the whole of the building could be contained within the observer's cone of vision. This increased distance between the building and the observer would, under normal conditions, allow greater visual penetration of the upper windows and an almost total elimination of sky reflection from them (166).

This should be obvious, because the greater distance will increase the angle between the visual ray and the windows, causing a reduction in reflections and a corresponding increase in visual penetration. Simple observation will confirm this, so it is sufficient to say that reflections on windows in renderings should be logical and used with extreme care.

166 Another diagram of an observer looking at a building, this time from a greater distance.

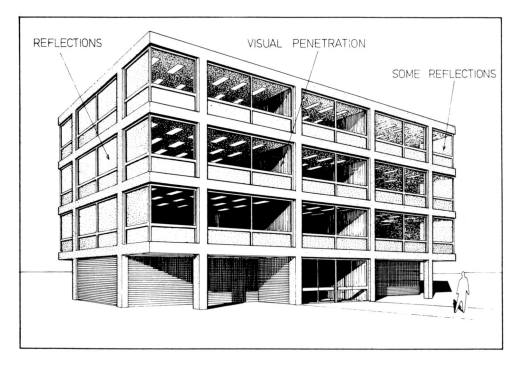

REFLECTIONS   VISUAL PENETRATION   SOME REFLECTIONS

167 A simple rendering of a small building.

This simplified example (**167**) shows that reflections occur on those windows that are at the smallest angles to the observer's sight lines, whilst visual penetration is restricted to those windows that are nearer to perpendicular to his sight lines.

When this elementary principle is applied to a much taller building, the reflection of the sky in the windows becomes stronger with increasing height. Because this building is located in a built-up area other buildings are reflected in the lower windows. The darker reflections of buildings allow greater visual penetration than the lighter sky reflection but at the scale of this illustration the visual penetration would be virtually impossible to show. Under these circumstances a compromise is accepted and these lower windows are shown dark and without interior detail.

A great deal can be learned from informed observation and once again the camera can be of inestimable value in studying the effects of light and shade, or shadow on glass, in varying locations and in differing relationships to the observer and the light source.

A slightly different problem is presented by smaller glass objects. For example, a drinking glass still has all of the properties of window glass, i.e. it is generally colourless, transparent and has reflective surfaces, but added to this it is a shaped hollow utensil usually based on a cylinder (**168**). Portraying a drinking glass is, therefore, basically a problem of visual penetration, reflections and, to a slightly lesser degree, of conventional light and shade.

168 Small glass objects still have the characteristics of window glass but because of their shape and size, they present added difficulties for the renderer.

The renderer's simplest approach to a drinking glass is the line drawing with a minimum of reflection and no light and shade. This is illustrated here (169) using four glasses; the suggestion of glass is offered by using a minimum of evidence, all of which indicates that the material is colourless, transparent and highly reflective.

169 Four drinking glasses.

A similar approach can be used for other glass objects such as a decanter, which is shown both empty and partially filled (170). Again, the glass is only suggested and the observer is given a minimum amount of evidence to confirm that the object is made of glass. The addition of a self-adhesive film with a highlight provides the suggestion of liquid in the decanter.

In each of these examples a sort of graphic shorthand is used to suggest glass rather than to render its texture. The fact that glass is transparent and colourless poses a considerable problem for the renderer, but fortunately its reflective surface is much easier to depict and it is this which must be portrayed in a rendering. The lighting of glass objects is very important and because glass also reflects images its placement and background are important.

170 Two versions of a decanter.

This illustration (**171**) demonstrates the value of a black background when rendering a glass decanter where dramatic contrasts of light and dark tones result in a convincing rendering.

This approach to rendering glass is of considerable value when dealing with objects made of decorative, or 'cut' glass (**172**). The unmistakable texture of the glass is mainly due to the strong contrasts between the reflected light and the dark background. The pattern of light and dark follows a simple logic. When the glass surfaces are more or less at right angles to the observer's line of sight he sees through the glass to the dark background. When the glass surfaces form acute angles with or are parallel to his line of sight, reflection takes over and he sees light tones.

173 A montage of glass objects.

This montage (173) shows a variety of fairly common examples of glass seen under various lighting conditions and with different backgrounds. The rendering of glass is an interesting and challenging subject with a number of special conditions which seem to contradict much of what has been discussed. Because of this it is worth repeating that if the basic principles are applied, together with careful observation, effective renderings of glass may be made.

174 Water being poured from a bottle.

Rendering water

Both water and glass are colourless, transparent and have reflecting surfaces. Perhaps the best way to introduce the similarities between rendering them is this illustration of water being poured from a bottle where both the glass and water have cylindrical shapes and, though the water is a moving liquid, the two different materials look almost identical (174). Renderings of this type are rarely required because water is usually seen in nature as a horizontal, smooth or rough surface, depending on a number of factors including weather conditions.

175 Canaletto's rendering of water in this view of the entrance to the Piazzetta, Venice, demonstrates how a simple technique based on careful observation can be very successful.

176 Depending on the viewing position, water can act as an almost perfect mirror, reflecting everything in position and correctly related to it and the observer.

Water with a completely smooth surface can be either transparent, as when contained in a swimming pool, or it can be an almost perfect mirror (176). Its appearance is dependent on the angle at which the smooth surface is seen, the depth of the water and the reflecting ability of the bottom. In fact, water offers the observer a large variety of effects depending on the conditions under which it is viewed. Because of the complexity of rendering water, only the basic approaches are considered here and, as with glass, they should be treated as a starting point because informed observation will show many variations. The wise renderer should look for and try to understand the reasons for those variations before accepting or rejecting them for depiction.

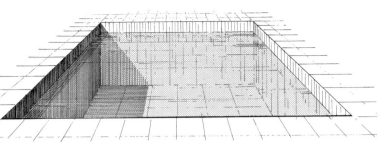

177 A simple example of undisturbed water in a swimming-pool.

When contained in a swimming-pool with an undisturbed surface, the water can be completely transparent, which is probably the easiest way to represent it in a rendering (**177**). The effect can be heightened in a coloured rendering if a light blue/green wash is applied to the surface of the water.

178 Reflections on the disturbed surface of water.

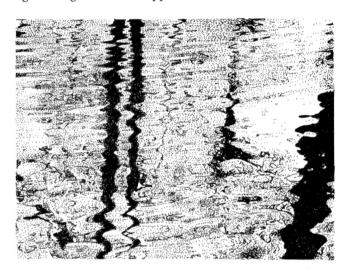

Reflections on the disturbed surface of water present a different effect (**178**).

179 An example of a choppy sea.

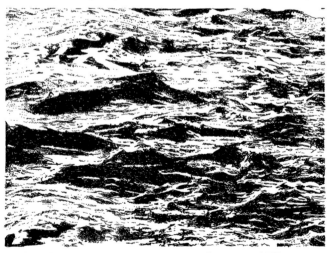

A choppy sea has a character all of its own (**179**).

These three illustrations show water under different conditions which result in very different 'textures'. Between complete transparency and almost perfect reflection is a vast range of different effects.

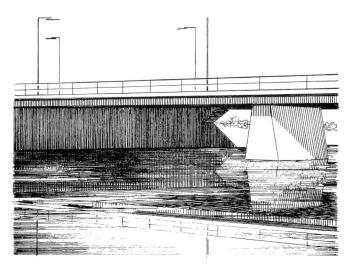

180 Impressions of water using horizontal lines, both ruled and freehand.

In the first of these two illustrations showing calm water (**180**) a ruled linear technique has been used. The second shows the building and the paving rendered with ruled lines and the water with freehand lines: because both are linear techniques no character conflict exists.

181 A montage of simple renderings of water.

Ruled and freehand lines used separately and in combination are included in these graphic approaches to rendering water (**181**). Effects vary from almost perfect mirror-image reflections to the absence of image reflection in rougher water. One example of unusual conditions is the fountain where water is forced under pressure into the air and allowed to fall freely, disturbing the surface of the pool.

Understanding the basic principles, informed observation and practice are the essentials for convincing renderings of water in any medium.

182 Renderings of water.

183 A montage of rocks.

VEDUTA del sotterraneo Fondamento del Mausoleo che fu eretto da Ele... Adriano Imp.... In questa parte, la qual e opposta alla Facciata, gli Speroni sono tutti a ...druiti di opera Travertina, cioe cosi sia di... A Parte di Riempitura, ovvero sia di... Opera incerta a cerci la quale veste d'ossi interno il Fondam. B Palizzate. C Parte del Mausoleo.

184
Giambattista Piranesi, *Foundations of the Castel San Angelo*, etching, 1756. This is a superb rendering of a massive stone structure in which the texture of the material is conveyed with great power.

Rendering rocks, brickwork and stonework

Because rocks vary so much in size, shape, texture and colour it is difficult to give specific instructions for rendering. The illustrations show rocks of various textures (**183**) and particular attention should be paid to the line of separation, because this is where the true character of the surface texture of any rock is identified. Once the character of the textures of various rocks is identified the rendering of rocks is considerably simplified.

185 Renderings of brickwork and stonework.

The same can be said of stonework and brickwork, for they too have distinctive textural characteristics. Again, the group of illustrations should help in identifying the true character of the textures of these materials (185).

Probably the most important consideration when rendering rocks, stonework and brickwork is the relationship between scale and detail. Naturally, the larger the scale the greater the detail required.

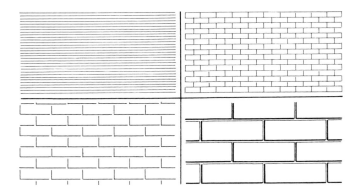

186 Approaches to brickwork on four different scales.

This is particularly true when rendering brickwork (186). The illusion of a third dimension adds interest in the two larger examples and examination of them should provide sufficient explanation of how this can be achieved. The direction of the light source must be considered when either of the two larger-scale techniques is used. Elevations of brickwork are shown, but their adaptation to perspective drawing can be achieved by using vanishing points for the horizontal lines and by applying the principles of fore-shortening.

187 Group of graphic renderings of stonework.

Stonework is approached in a similar way to brickwork and again the amount of detail is dependent on the scale of the drawing. The illustration (187) shows some simple self-explanatory graphic approaches to representing stonework.

188 Natural rocks, brickwork and concrete form the materials for this Davis Bité rendering of St Mary's Catholic Church, Lanchester, Pennsylvania.

Any material can be successfully rendered if the true nature of its texture is recognized and accurately reproduced in the required medium or technique. The number of different materials and textures is so great that it is impossible to deal with all of them here, but a few of the more important ones are included to help students with their own research.

189 Different materials are rendered with considerable power in this interior of Holocaust Memorial Museum, Washington, D.C., drawn by Paul Stevenson Oles in 1987.

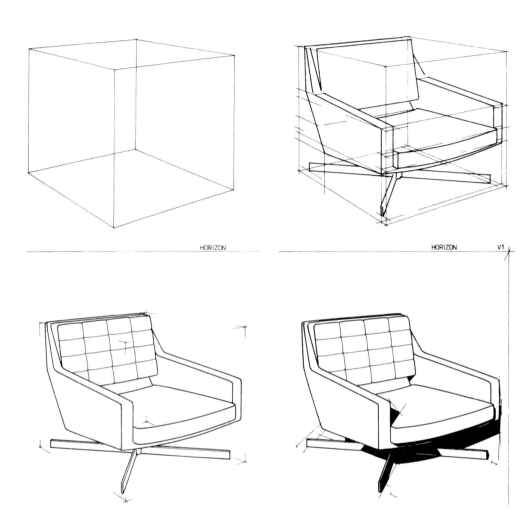

190 A perspective drawing of a chair, from box to shadow projection.

Rendering leather, fabrics and floor coverings

A rendering of an object such as a chair should be based on an accurate perspective drawing and a correct tonal interpretation to show the shape and should also show the type of upholstery, such as leather or fabric, in order to convey all of the essential information about the chair.

The chair has been set up using the 'Box Method' for drawing objects in perspective (**190**). This consists of 'placing' the object in a containing box which is drawn in perspective and, by using dimensions from the orthographic projection, the unwanted parts of the box are removed to leave the required chair shape.

When the perspective drawing of the chair is completed, a light source is chosen and the shadow shapes constructed, together with the light and shade pattern and the line of separation. When all of these are completed the drawing is ready for rendering in any required medium or technique.

191 Fabric- and leather-covered chairs.

192 Lighter versions of fabric- and leather-covered chairs.

The 'softer' look of the fabric-covered chair is mainly because of the reduced contrast between the tones and the elimination of reflected highlights, together with a rendering technique that helps to suggest the weave or character of the fabric (**191**). Compare this 'softer' look of the fabric with the 'harder' look of the leather-covered chair. Both of these chairs are covered in dark material, which makes it comparatively easy to produce a fairly dramatic result.

The same chair covered with lighter versions of the same materials presents a slightly more difficult problem, because the lighter tones do not allow the renderer to work with the same large range of values. These lighter materials do not alter the texture or the illusion of a third dimension but are rendered using lighter tones and reduced contrasts (**192**).

193 Two chairs with different coverings.

From these examples it can be seen that different fabric textures and colours can be produced without compromising the shape of the chair and the illusion of a third dimension. Expressing the shape of the chair is fundamental to a successful rendering. The basic tonal pattern will still apply irrespective of the chair's colour or texture, but will be modified by the type of upholstery. Once the character of the upholstery is identified it can be reproduced without undue difficulty (**193**).

194 Detail of a leather-covered cushion.

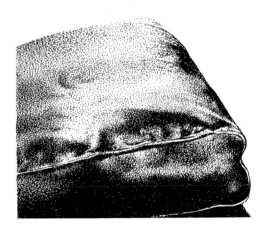

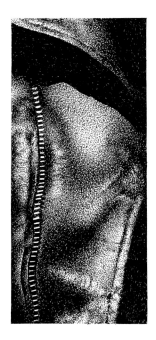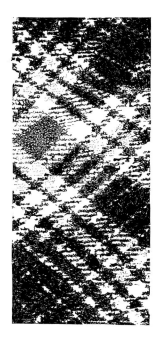

So far only fabric and leather or vinyl upholstery stretched over the contours of a chair have been considered. Both of these types of material have many other uses: upholstery leather, for example, instead of being stretched over the contours of the chair, might be used to cover loose cushions giving a softer, 'sat-in' look. This 'comfortable' look is suggested by changing the hard, precise edges and the evenly graded tones. Instead, softer edges are achieved with more flowing lines and the surfaces are broken up to represent light and shade on an uneven surface (**194**).

Informed observation of the character of a material is of approximately equal importance to knowledge of the basic principles when producing textures in renderings. Unless this true character is accurately assessed, satisfactory results can seldom be obtained in a rendering irrespective of the medium or technique.

Leather and vinyl, whether used for clothing or chairs, still retain their characteristic differences from fabric. These three details indicate the different characters of the textures of leather and fabric when used for clothes (**195**). The 'harder' reflective surface of the leather is contrasted with the 'softer' woven look of the two fabrics, which are not reflective to the same degree.

195 A section of leather and two kinds of fabric.

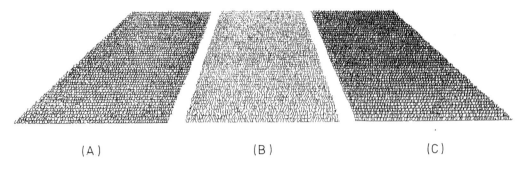

(A)   (B)   (C)

196 Carpet textures.

Another area where the character of a texture needs careful observation is floor coverings. In particular, carpets need special attention if good representations are to be made in interior renderings. Three different useful textures are demonstrated (**196**), all of which use similar techniques to produce different believable carpet textures.

These carpet textures are produced with freehand lines drawn using a straight-edge as a guide. Example 'A' is a series of 'u's strung together, 'B' consists of short vertical or near vertical lines, while 'C' consists of strings of 'e's; all are in more or less continuous lines. Perspective in each case is achieved by varying the spacing between the lines as necessary and this variation can also be used in conjunction with a reduction or an increase in the density of the lines themselves to produce an atmospheric effect. The density of the lines is also used to portray darker or lighter tones of these carpet textures.

197 Shadows shown by introducing intermediate lines.

Shadows cast on these carpet textures can be produced by introducing an intermediate line of the same units between those of the original texture. The example (**197**) shows how this is done without destroying the character of the carpet texture or the transparent quality of the shadow which is consistent with reality. These are by no means all of the carpet textures which can be used, but they are very useful for general carpet representations.

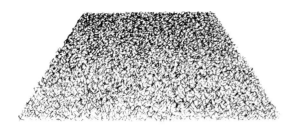

More specialized carpet textures can be produced by careful observation and some intelligent experimentation. For example, the much longer pile carpet shown here (198) has a very distinctive character which is a little more difficult to produce than the other types.

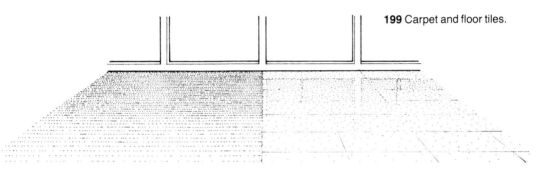

199 Carpet and floor tiles.

The difference between carpet and other forms of floor coverings, e.g. floor tiles, can be shown easily by recognizing the different characters of the two materials and expressing those differences in the rendering. This simple example (199) demonstrates the difference in character between the non-reflective carpet and the reflective floor tiles. There are many other floor coverings of different materials in common use, but as most are either non-reflective or reflective they can be reproduced in a rendering fairly easily if the texture's character is accurately assessed. Whilst floor textures are tedious to reproduce because of the large areas usually involved, they are among the easiest textures to render.

Only the most important, frequently needed textures have been examined in detail, but a number of others can be found in the montages of renderings of various textures.

From this section on rendering textures it can be seen how closely they are identified with value and how dependent they are on the same principles. Value contrasts are very important factors in rendering, irrespective of the particular graphic field because, if the value contrasts are carefully controlled, the illusion of a third dimension is increased considerably. Though important, neither a correctly drawn perspective nor a carefully constructed colour harmony can achieve the illusion of a third dimension in a rendering unless the values are correctly interpreted.

149

200 and **201** (opposite) Montages of textures.

202 Montage – industry.

The following illustrations (**202, 203, 204**) show different textures applied to various objects. Tubular drawing pens were used in various ways including a stipple tech-

nique, a multidirectional linear technique and a simple blacking-in technique, but satisfactory results can be produced in any medium using any suitable technique.

203 Montage – transport.

204 A variety of textures.

Dry-transfer and self-adhesive materials

The introduction of dry-transfer material in the 1960s and the self-adhesive screen a few years earlier brought about a revolution which had enormous impact on the whole field of graphics. A very large number of typefaces in different sizes and colours, symbols, trees, people, cars and trucks, food, animals, world landmarks, etc. as well as a large range of other graphic materials including a comprehensive range of self-adhesive screens in black, white and various colours are available. Products of consistently high quality are available from Letraset International Limited, London, and Mecanorma Industries, France; complete catalogues are available from Letraset and Mecanorma dealers throughout the world.

Skill-building exercises

One of the best ways to learn anything is to do it and students are advised to start with some renderings of simple objects. It is important to work from simple examples and master them before moving on to more advanced ones. Students following this logical progression will find that their knowledge and skills are soundly built and more satisfying results are achieved.

205 The impressive skills
exhibited by Paul
Stevenson Oles in his
interior rendering for the
National Gallery,
Washington, D.C., are
typical of those that have
placed him among the
great modern delineators.

157

206 Line drawings of three cubes.

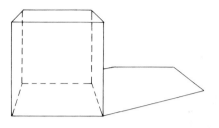

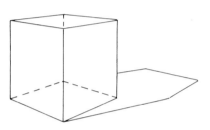

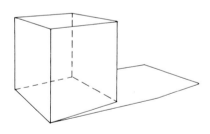

The programme should be commenced by rendering some simple cubes and three suitable examples are shown here (**206**). Each cube should be copied and rendered using 2H, H, HB, B, 2B, 4B and 6B pencils until the necessary skills are developed.

There should be no visible lines at the changes of direction of planes in the finished rendering. The changes of direction should be shown by contrast in the values of the surfaces.

HORIZONTAL SURFACE
RENDERED HORIZONTALLY

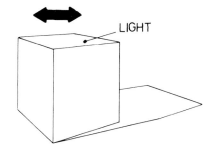

LIGHT

207 Line drawings of a
cube showing the direction
in which each plane should
be rendered.

VERTICAL SURFACES
RENDERED VERTICALLY

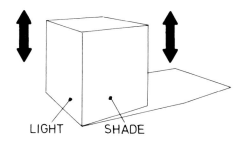

LIGHT   SHADE

HORIZONTAL SURFACE IN SHADOW
RENDERED HORIZONTALLY

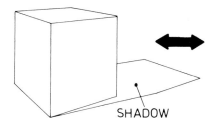

SHADOW

Always render in the direction of the plane, i.e. a horizontal plane should be rendered horizontally and a vertical plane should be rendered vertically (**207**). This accentuates the direction of the plane and is a subtle reinforcement of the visual message. In a slightly more practical way, rendering in the direction of the plane is logical, because all dynamic planes are subject to atmospheric effect, so there will be subtle gradation in their values. This gradation is most easily expressed in linear techniques by rendering in the direction of the plane. If this basic rule is applied the rendering process becomes much easier and more effective.

208 Four renderings based on a cube.

When some competence is achieved in rendering simple cubes, the next step should be to attempt slightly more complex shapes of this type (**208**). These projects are very useful in building an understanding of the principles involved and, if enough examples are completed using the correct principles, the essential skills can be considerably improved.

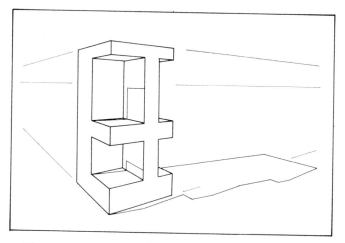

The next exercise should be rendering slightly larger and more complex shapes such as this cut block (**209**). The reason for using a cut block is to help students to build a better understanding of the illusion of the third dimension in two-dimensional representations. If students begin the project with a solid block and have to cut and remove parts, the necessity of showing what is left gives them a much better idea of the reality of the solids and spaces being represented.

Remember that time spent on the preparation of a drawing for rendering is never wasted because an accurate perspective drawing, correct shadow projection, a carefully identified line of separation and correctly identified light and shade are essential to a good rendering. Without this realistic basis it does not matter how skilfully the rendering is done, for the finished work will lack the credibility essential to good graphic communication.

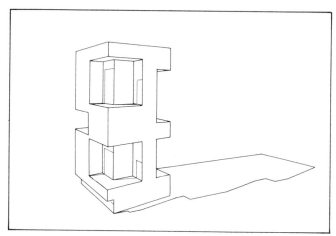

210 A more complex line drawing of a cut block.

This slightly more complex example (**210**) is shown first as a line drawing, which is based on a correctly set up perspective drawing with a carefully placed light source and accurately constructed shadow shapes.

211 A cut block rendered in pen and ink.

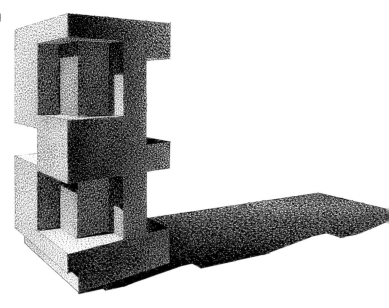

The finished rendering (**211**) shows the value of this careful preparation and is the result of using all of the aspects discussed.

Please note that all of the illustrations explaining the principles in this book have been done using tubular pens because this medium and technique reproduces with stronger contrast than pencil and therefore makes the illustrations more useful to the student. Nevertheless, with practice, pencils can be used to produce renderings of very high quality.

Although only a limited number of objects have been used for demonstration purposes, any subject can be rendered using the principles discussed. Irrespective of the subject, the medium or the technique the basic requirements remain the same.

These two 'Space Constructions' (**212, 213**) will help to make the transition from single shapes in space to multiple shapes within a picture area. Students are advised either to copy these drawings or make their own based on these ideas. A correct perspective drawing must be made and a suitable light source chosen with the shadow shapes constructed and the lines of separation and the light and shade faces identified. The rendering must be carried out in accordance with the tonal pattern and atmospheric effect, and the planes must be rendered in the appropriate direction.

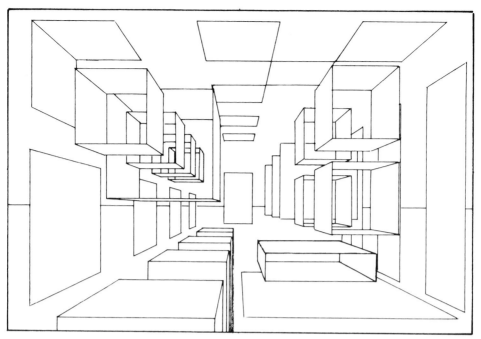

Pencils should be used for these exercises, which should be done not larger than about A4 size. Though both pencil and pen-and-ink can be used by experienced artists for large drawings, the beginner is advised not to attempt work on a large scale because it is time-consuming, extremely demanding and seldom achieves anything which cannot be achieved with smaller drawings.

212 and **213** Two space constructions.

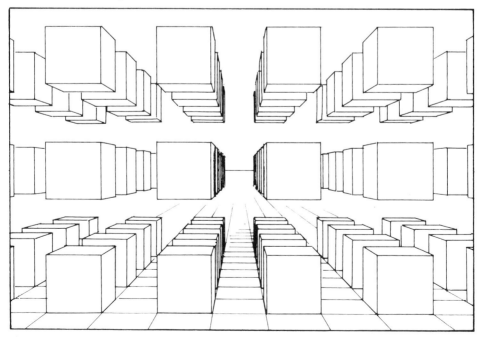

214 Objects based on cylinders.

When shapes made up of flat surfaces have been mastered students should move on to objects with curved surfaces, e.g. cylinders and cones and, later, spheres. These shapes are particularly demanding, but if the basic principles are followed, they will be made considerably easier. The examples shown (**214**) are objects based on cylinders and though different materials are depicted, the basic principles have been followed.

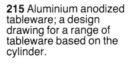

215 Aluminium anodized tableware; a design drawing for a range of tableware based on the cylinder.

This group of cylindrical objects (215) has semi-reflective exterior surfaces and dark-toned, matt interior surfaces which the renderings show to advantage. None of the objects exists as anything more than an idea in the form of design drawings and because of this it was not possible to make the drawings from direct observation of the actual objects. However, by using the basic principles and observation of other similar objects it was possible to create graphic representations of these objects as they would appear in reality.

Both the designer and the artist are frequently faced with producing graphic images of objects and views which do not exist in any real form. They must be able to portray objects which exist only in the imagination or as orthographic projections, i.e. plans, elevations and sections. Without knowledge of the basic principles and developed skills the designer or artist is severely limited in any attempt to convince the observer of the reality of the objects or views depicted.

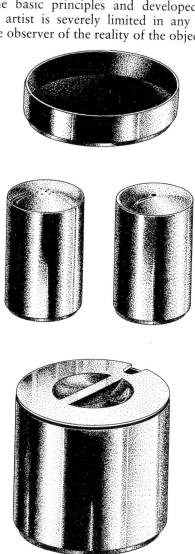

216 Rendering of a Chinon 410 Macro Zoom movie camera.

The rendering of the movie camera in this illustration (**216**) was done from an actual object and although direct observation was possible the basic principles were still very important. When making this type of rendering it is often very difficult to achieve lighting conditions that show all of the aspects of the object to advantage. In such cases direct observation is of some value, but knowledge of the basic principles is essential to complete the rendering. In other words, it is necessary to combine what is seen with what is known and in this way the two-dimensional image of the three-dimensional object can be made.

217 Rendering of an elevation of a steam locomotive.

This is a rendering of an elevation of a steam locomotive (**217**) and though the locomotive does exist it would be impossible to see this view of it. Any object in reality, irrespective of the viewing position, will be seen affected by perspective. Though this drawing is only an elevation (a diagram showing actual measured proportions) in which no perspective principles have been used, the addition of rendering has introduced a powerful illusion of a three-dimensional reality to show the locomotive to advantage. Such drawings can be very effective in conveying accurate information about objects while also showing that the objects have three-dimensions, without actually showing them affected by perspective.

The illustration of the movie projector (**218**) is another example of an elevation being rendered to add a simple illusion of reality with the emphasis on the technical information. Though this type of drawing is extremely useful for the communication of certain types of graphic information, it is only one of a number of methods which can be used. Other methods include orthographic projection, isometric projection, isometric drawing, axonometric projection, all four oblique projections (cabinet, cavalier, alternative cabinet and alternative cavalier projections), dimetric, trimetric and perspective projections (one-point, two-point and three-point constructions).

218 Copal Sekonic CP77 movie projector.

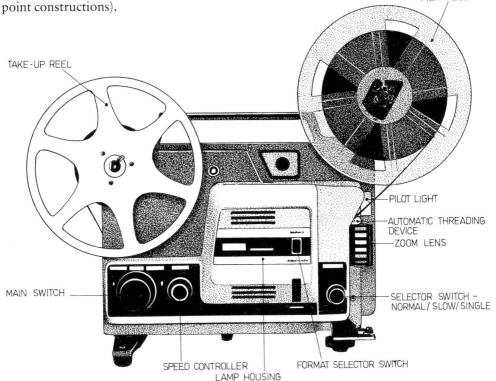

FILM REEL

TAKE-UP REEL

PILOT LIGHT

AUTOMATIC THREADING DEVICE

ZOOM LENS

MAIN SWITCH

SELECTOR SWITCH – NORMAL / SLOW/ SINGLE

SPEED CONTROLLER

LAMP HOUSING

FORMAT SELECTOR SWITCH

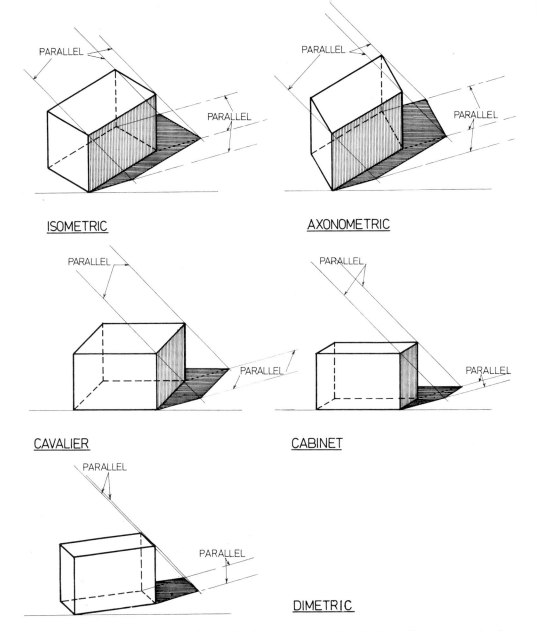

ISOMETRIC

AXONOMETRIC

CAVALIER

CABINET

DIMETRIC

219 Shadow projection on different metric projections. In each of these examples the light rays are parallel, as are their plans. Shadows cast by the object in each of the projections are constructed using the same basic method as is used in orthographic shadow projection (sciagraphy), as shown previously.

The methods for constructing shadow shapes on each of the metric projections are not discussed here because the diagrams should be self-explanatory (**219**). Further information can be found in *Creative Perspective*.

Probably the most popular method of showing graphic representations of objects is the rendered perspective drawing. This illustration shows a number of simply rendered perspective drawings of different types of slide projectors and a sectional 'view' of another (**220**). Though these are all simple renderings they convey the visual message with a clarity and directness that is extremely difficult to produce in any other way. Even a photograph is, in some cases, limited in what it can show when it is used to convey detailed information.

Often the photographer is faced with an almost insoluble problem when photographing some objects because if the object is lit so that its shape is clearly portrayed, detail can be lost in some areas and if it is lit so that detail is portrayed the shape can be lost. The renderer is not restricted in this way because he can choose a light source to emphasize the shape of the object and then control the value relationships to show the required detail.

220 The slide projector.

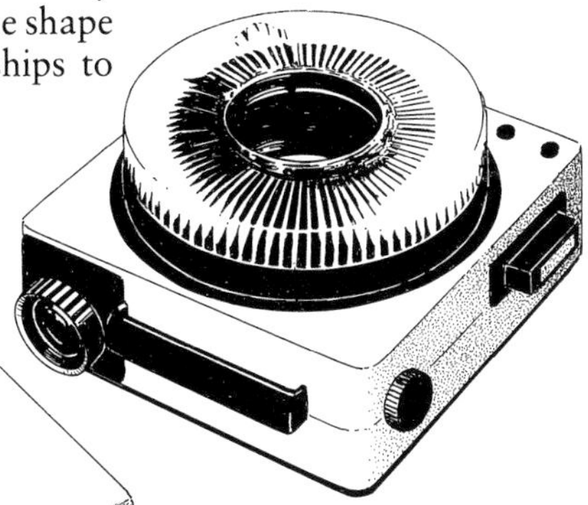

KODAK S-AV 2000 PROJECTOR

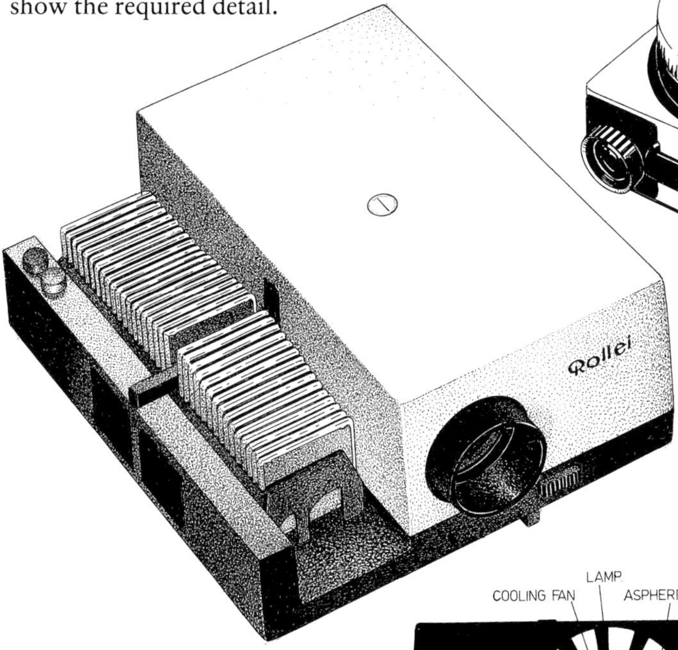

ROLLEI P35 A PROJECTOR

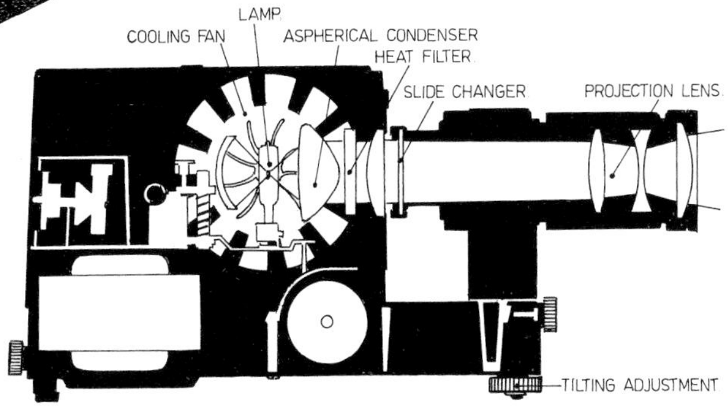

COOLING FAN   LAMP   ASPHERICAL CONDENSER

HEAT FILTER

SLIDE CHANGER   PROJECTION LENS

TILTING ADJUSTMENT

LEITZ – PRADO–UNIVERSAL PROJECTOR

HITACHI SPS-1215R SOUND PROJECTOR

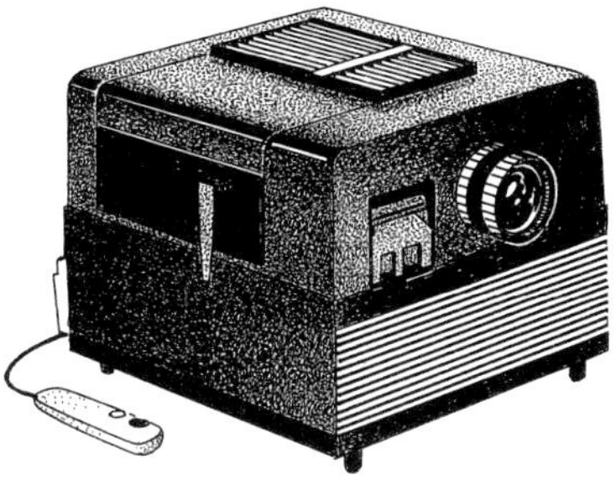

ZEISS IKON – PERKEO AV502 AUDIO-VISUAL PROJECTOR

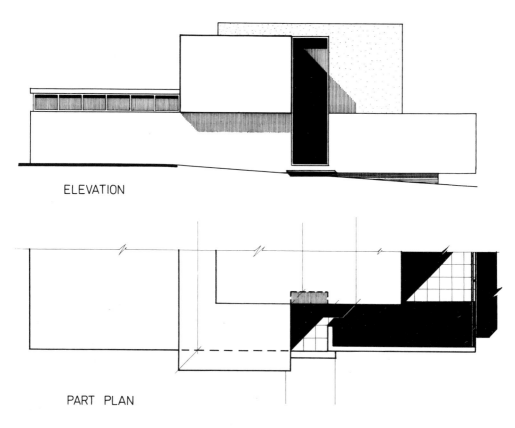

ELEVATION

PART PLAN

221 An elevation and part plan of a simple building with shadows.

Sciagraphy

This illustration (**221**) shows another method of indicating an illusion of the third dimension on an orthographic projection. In this case, a plan and an elevation of a simple building are used and the illusion of a third dimension is introduced by using the principles of sciagraphy to project shadows on these diagrams. Sciagraphy is the science of constructing shadow shapes on orthographic projections. This shadow projection is carried out by establishing the direction of the parallel light rays from the sun in relation to the plan, and their angle of elevation in relation to the elevation of the building. It is not intended to elaborate the principles of sciagraphy here (they can be found in specialist reference books), but their use to portray the illusion of a third dimension is an important aspect of rendering.

The illustration opposite (**222**) is a typical example of the use of sciagraphy to introduce an illusion of a third dimension. The lengths of the various shadows show the related heights of the buildings in this area development. Without the shadow shapes the drawing would be flat and very difficult for the inexperienced observer to read. Architectural and landscape subjects are only two of many for which the renderer can use the principles of sciagraphy to improve clarity and add interest.

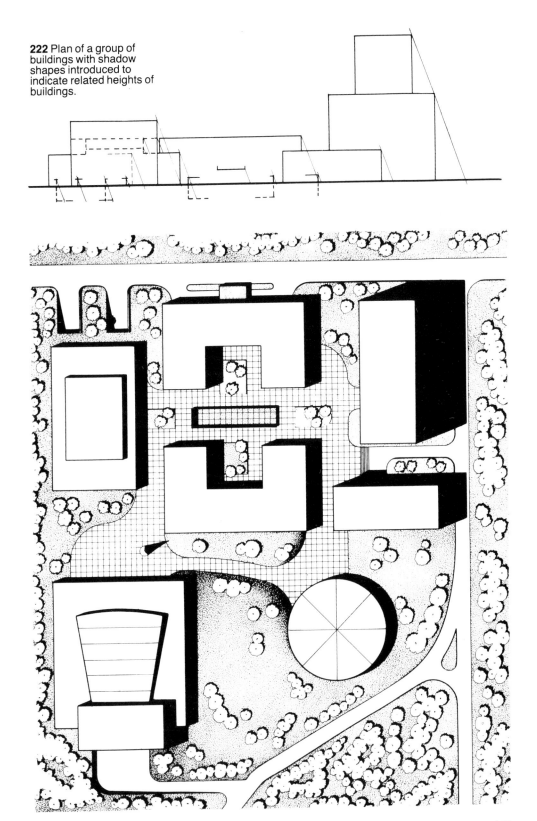

222 Plan of a group of buildings with shadow shapes introduced to indicate related heights of buildings.

223 'Sculpture'.

The illusion of a third dimension has been introduced into an otherwise flat drawing (**223**). This approach can be used for many different subjects with many different effects and the only limiting factors are the imagination and skill of the designer or artist.

The principles of sciagraphy have been used to construct the shade and shadow shapes of these plans of objects grouped together to form a pattern (**224**). The light and shade parts of the shapes and their shadows have been rendered in accordance with the principles of atmospheric effect to introduce the illusion of a third dimension. Simple exercises of this type are of great benefit when developing rendering skills and though the results may lack some of the excitement of more creative designs they do reinforce a valuable point.

In this slightly more imaginative design (**225**), static planes of different shapes and sizes have been rendered to create the illusion of different levels within the picture area. There are no recognizable linear elements of perspective in this design and it is the cast shadows in conjunction with the principles of atmospheric effect and the overlapping that are the major factors responsible for the strong illusion of a third dimension.

224 Plans of shapes rendered using sciagraphy.

225 Abstract design using static planes and sciagraphy.

226 Rembrandt van Rijn used overlapping in his 1645 etching *The Omval* to increase the illusion of space and distance.

Overlapping

In this example (**227**), illustration A shows six panels and because there is no indication of a depth relationship it is assumed that they are all laid on a flat surface. Illustration B shows the same six panels rearranged so that some are in front of others, which means that there must be a third dimension involved, no matter how small it might be. In this very simple way, overlapping implies a third dimension.

If shadow shapes are added to the overlapping panels, not only is the third dimension implied, but it is possible to establish that the panels are placed at different distances apart, thus confirming the illusion of a third dimension (**228**). Illustration C shows the shadow shapes when the panels are placed at different distances from a vertical back panel. (Sciagraphy has been used to construct the shadow shapes.) Illustration D shows the shadow shapes when the panels are placed vertically on a horizontal base plane. (The three-dimensional shadow construction has been used for the shadow shapes in this example.)

This illustration (**229**) shows the same panels rendered in accordance with the principles of atmospheric effect, which has been slightly exaggerated to illustrate the point. The introduction of related values has increased the illusion of the third dimension. This simple exercise shows that overlapping, shadow projection and the use of atmospheric effect all contribute to the overall illusion.

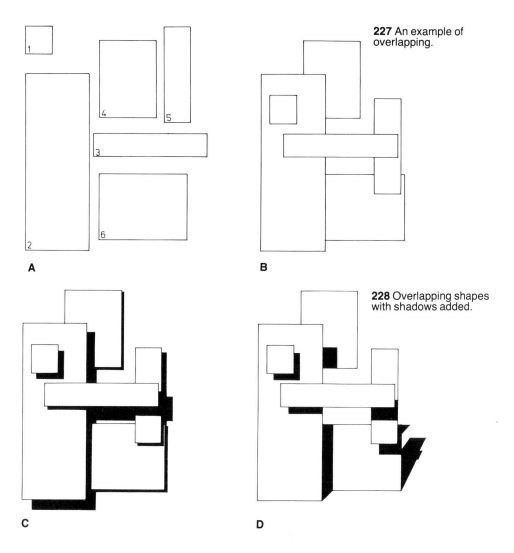

227 An example of overlapping.

A

B

228 Overlapping shapes with shadows added.

C

D

229 Rendered overlapping planes.

230 In this 1744 etching by Canaletto entitled *Arch with a Lantern*, all of the elements are brought together by a master draughtsman and the result is an extremely powerful communication.

Getting it all together

At this point it is important that all of the material discussed in this book be brought together and consolidated in a simple example which uses many of the principles essential to the creation of the illusion of the third dimension.

231 A finished drawing of three men.

When all of the optical laws are introduced into a simple drawing, such as this one (**231**), the illusion of the third dimension is convincing. The three men, dressed in an identical fashion, are placed at increasing distances from the observer.

The first optical law states that receding parallel lines appear to converge to a common point. This is known as convergence (**232**). If those parallel lines are in the horizontal plane, the common point known as the vanishing point will be located in the horizon line. The use of this optical law introduces the first evidence of the third dimension.

The second optical law concerns foreshortening and states that equal distances appear to diminish in size as the distance from the observer increases (**233**). This is demonstrated by the lateral paving joints, which appear closer together as the distance from the observer increases. Though this process must go on as long as the pavement is seen, in this example the lateral joints have been omitted after a certain distance, because observation shows that they will gradually disappear from view. With the introduction of foreshortening the illusion of the third dimension is reinforced.

232 Convergence.

HORIZON LINE   VANISHING POINT

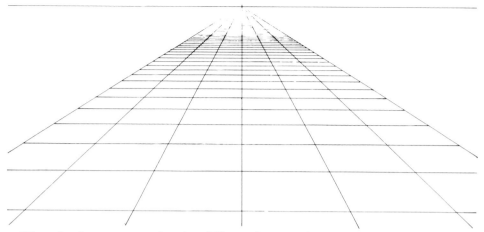

When the three men are placed at different distances from the observer, the third optical law which concerns diminution is apparent (234). This law states that objects of the same size will appear smaller as the distance increases. The three men are the same size, so as the distance increases the size of the man portrayed is decreased. Diminution can also be identified in the receding lines where the spaces between these lines appear to diminish as the distance increases. The foreshortening of the lateral pavement joints can be described as the diminishing of the spaces between the lateral lines as the distance increases. With the introduction of diminution the illusion of the third dimension is further reinforced.

It should be noted at this point that the three figures have been carefully placed so that the front one overlaps the second. By introducing overlapping, though technically it is not a basic optical law, the illusion of the third dimension is increased considerably. The optical logic of overlapping is that for something to be in front of something else there must be space or depth between the two.

233 Foreshortening.

234 Diminution.

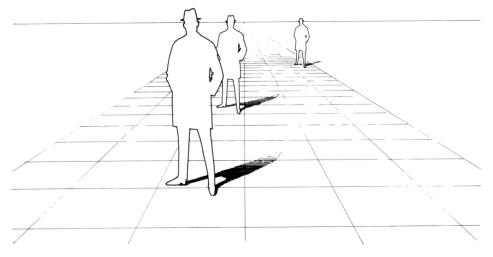

235 Shade and Shadow.

Light is the basis of all seeing, so it must play an extremely important role in drawing and painting. When light, shade and shadow are introduced, the illusion of the third dimension is considerably increased (**235**). To keep this drawing simple the light source has been chosen to concentrate the shade on the backs of the figures, so it does not play any role in this picture.

When the figures are simply rendered they will be subject to atmospheric effect, which results in both light and dark values neutralizing as the distance from the observer increases. All surfaces seen in the picture will be subject to atmospheric effect, so the base plane including the pavement joints and the shadows cast by the three figures will appear to neutralize as distance increases (**236**).

Additional elements contributing to the illusion of the third dimension are contrast and detail, but they are closely related to the optical laws already discussed. For example, the greatest detail and the greatest contrast between tones is in the foreground, i.e. closest to the observer's eye, and as the distance increases the detail and the contrast appear to decrease. This is consistent with the principles of atmospheric effect.

236 Atmospheric effect.

From this simple exercise, it can be seen that the illusion of the third dimension is produced by the interaction of convergence, foreshortening, diminution, light, shade and shadow, atmospheric effect and overlapping. If understanding and skill are applied to the use of these essential aspects in a drawing or painting the result will be greatly improved.

Examples of renderings

The following examples cover a variety of subjects, all of which rely to a greater or lesser extent on the knowledge of the basic principles and skills discussed in this book.

237 A rendering of a tree.

Trees

This pen-and-ink drawing of a tree (**237**) was done using a traditional pen-and-ink technique. Trees are good subjects for learning rendering because they are almost endless in their variety, as are the techniques and media for rendering them. In rendering trees, the main problem, apart from producing the correct shape, is making the tree look 'round', i.e. three-dimensional. Probably the best advice to beginners is to go out and look at trees and try to reproduce what is seen. This is preferable to trying to draw trees from memory or imagination because such trees too frequently appear flat and two-dimensional.

238 Exterior view of a building.

Architecture

The architectural renderer, known as a delineator or perspectivist, when faced with the rendering of a building has one of the most complex of all rendering problems. Apart from being able to solve all of the more obvious problems, such as where to place the observer, what size to make the drawing, what medium to use, the most suitable technique and how much of the surroundings to include, he must be competent at both drawing and rendering such diverse

objects as trees, people, cars, landscapes, lakes and the sea. He must also be competent at rendering materials such as brick, stone, steel, concrete, glass and plastics. All of this he must be able to carry out within the overall framework of a correct perspective drawing on which the precise shadow shapes are constructed together with atmospheric effect and contrast, etc., introduced according to optical reality so that the final rendering presents the true intent of the design (**238**).

239 Space structure.

This space construction with a figure (**239**) uses the same basic optical principles and skills to create the illusion of the third dimension. This type of drawing provides good practice in setting up simple objects in perspective and constructing their shadow shapes, which form a solid foundation for the picture. The choice of a light source is very important, as is subtle rendering of the atmospheric effect.

Light and shade, texture and contrast are used to render this detail from an old wall (**240**). The photographic quality of this rendering is the result of a stipple pen-and-ink technique, which is closer to the printer's screen-printing techniques than the more traditional pen line technique. Pencil or any other medium can be used for this type of drawing if a suitable technique is adopted, because it is not so much the medium as the application of the optical principles that is responsible for the result.

240 Detail from an old wall.

241 Richard Burton.

242 Charles Aznavour.

Portraiture

This rendering of the late Richard Burton (**241**) relies on the same technique and application of the optical principles as the previous illustration. Stronger contrasts have been used to produce a more dramatic result.

The portrayal of singer Charles Aznavour (**242**) was rendered using contrasts similar to those in the previous example. By controlling the contrasts in the drawing within the basic optical laws almost any desired effect can be achieved. This control of contrasts is similar to the photographer's control of the lighting of a subject and the printing of a photograph. The renderer can control the lighting conditions from harsh, resulting in 'high key' drawings like those of Richard Burton and Charles Aznavour, to a softer lighting condition resulting in a 'low key' drawing such as the wall detail, or any desired variation between these effects.

243 Louis Armstrong.

This rendering of the great American jazz musician, Louis Armstrong, is included because it is an example of a drawing that relies on the portrayal of a number of different textures (**243**). The same stipple pen-and-ink technique was used as for most of the other drawings in this segment. The contrast in texture between the black skin, the fabric of the clothes and the highly polished metal of the trumpet was achieved without changing the technique.

Imagination

This example (244) is a more abstract drawing which, in spite of its lack of realism in one sense, still relies on the basic optical rules for its illusion of the third dimension. Contrast provides the pattern and, with a little help from 'light and shade', an observer is led into and around the rendering where elements are located in space. Short multidirectional lines were used for this rendering.

244 Semi-abstract pattern.

245 Abstract pattern.

246 Abstract pattern.

The abstract pattern in this illustration (**245**) is another example of the effects that can be produced with a stipple technique. Complex designs such as this rely very strongly on knowledge of the optical laws and basic rendering skills which are used, and in some cases distorted and/or exaggerated to heighten the overall three-dimensional effect. This statement that optical laws and rendering skills can be distorted should not be misunderstood or used as an excuse for ignoring the valid picture-making processes. Basic principles and laws can be extended or distorted to achieve a required result only if it is done with considerable care and proper compensations are made. Many great artists appear to break the rules frequently and with very successful results, but what is not so obvious are the compensations they make for these apparently broken rules. It is very risky to break rules in art, graphics and design, because the rules must be fully understood before they can be interfered with in any way if a successful result is expected.

The possibilities for development of this type of rendering are virtually endless (**246**), but all of the principles discussed in this book are just as essential in this type of work as in any other.

Style

Style, which is an important aspect of drawing, rendering and painting, is part of the artist's or designer's integrity. *The Thames and Hudson Encyclopaedia of the Arts*, edited by the late Sir Herbert Read, states that 'Style is the term for the manner of execution in writing, painting, etc. as opposed to subject matter or its organization (i.e., form); (2) The common characteristics of the arts in a given period – e.g. Louis XIV – or of a school or movement.' It is important to understand that style is quite independent of medium or technique. In other words, style is the individual way an artist or designer uses the valid principles and real developed skills to express himself in a way which makes his work unique. A lack of individual style built on valid principles and real developed skills tends to make people working in art and design into little more than human photocopiers.

Perhaps the best way to gain an understanding of the importance of style to the artist or designer is to examine the drawings of the masters in different areas of art and design.

In the group of drawings that follows each artist or designer is an individual and though in some cases their subjects are similar, each has made a drawing in his or her own individual style. It is this style which makes an artist's work immediately recognizable, because each has an individual way of expressing his or her ideas. When this is added to the obvious exhibited knowledge of the basic principles of communicating with graphics and the undoubted master craftsmanship in the chosen medium, each work is rightly identified as that of a master.

247 Style is the element
that identifies a drawing or
painting as the work of a
specific artist. For example,
it would be difficult to
mistake this drawing of the
Bust of a Warrior by
Leonardo Da Vinci for the
work of anyone else.

248 The individual style of
Albrecht Dürer is evident in
this well-known charcoal
drawing of his mother
which he did in 1514,
shortly before her death.

194

249 (opposite) This 1509 chalk drawing by Raphael, *Study for the Figure of Poetry*, illustrates well the difference in style between the work of Raphael and, say, Leonardo Da Vinci. Raphael's drawing is made from a knowledge of the surface of the figure but Da Vinci's (**247**) is built on a knowledge of the structure.

250 Rembrandt's drawings are built on remarkable powers of observation and an economy of drawing which gives his work an excitingly spontaneous look, as in this brush drawing entitled *A Woman Asleep*.

251 Edgar Degas made
drawings that have a solid
three-dimensional
appearance, expressing
form and life as though one
was dependent on the
other, as shown here in a
pastel drawing of 1885,
The Bath.

252 Paul Cézanne's ability
to convey the structure of
his subject matter gives his
work an almost sculptural
sense of permanence. In
this painting entitled *Dr
Gachet's House*, the
perspective of the twisting
road leads our eye to the
focal point of the picture.

modigliani

253 Though Modigliani's portraits were often strange his ability as a brilliant draughtsman cannot be questioned. His drawings have a sureness which allows him the luxury of distortion and economy.

254 In this 1919 lithograph, Egon Schiele's emotionally charged handling of line gives the picture a disturbing tension.

255 Käthe Kollwitz showed in her powerful self-portrait of 1934 that she was able to achieve something that is extremely rare in art. Her remarkable achievement was to fuse the image of a likeness with a feeling of a woman worn out by caring too much for those whose problems she shouldered.

Final Statement

It is worth repeating the basic philosophy developed in the beginning of this book, which is that 'Graphics is a means of communication and therefore, to be valid it must communicate.' It reasonably follows that graphics must have a common language, otherwise its value will be questionable. Any student with a serious desire to achieve a high degree of excellence in art, graphics, design or photography must be prepared to accept the rigid discipline required to learn the fundamental principles of literacy in pictorial communication. He or she must learn to see and interpret what is seen in an effective way. Some of the material included in this introduction to basic rendering has been dealt with only briefly and it is acknowledged that there is a great deal more. Before advanced aspects of the subject can be of any real value, the principles must be learnt and understood, because only then is it possible to begin drawing what you see the way you see it.

Rendering is a very large and complex subject which requires a great deal of study and practice before high-quality results can be achieved. It cannot be emphasized too often that there is no substitute for valid knowledge, real developed skills and accumulated experience as the basis for competence in art, graphics and design. A study of the history of Western art shows that all of the great artists and designers have exhibited outstanding knowledge, skills to virtuoso craftsmanship levels and a lifetime of experience, all of which are evident in their mature works.

Glossary

AERIAL PERSPECTIVE The representation of space by gradations of colour and value that parallel the effect produced by various densities of air on the appearance of objects.

ARCHITECTURAL DELINEATOR One who makes graphic representations of buildings for design evaluation or design communication.

ATMOSPHERIC EFFECT The effect caused by pollutants suspended in the atmosphere.

ATMOSPHERIC UMBRELLA The reflective capacity of the sky due to suspended pollutants.

CENTRE LINE OF VISION The direct line of sight of an observer located at the station point in a perspective construction.

COMPOSITION The formal arrangement of a painting or work of graphic art.

CONE OF VISION The limit of clear vision of the human eye when held perfectly still. This limit is established by research as a maximum angle of sixty degrees.

CONTRAST A combination of opposites or nearly opposite qualities; opposition, unlikeness, variety, conflict.

CONVERGENCE The approach to a common point. The opposite of radiation. Lines or edges which in reality are parallel appear to come together or converge as they recede from the observer.

DESIGN The art of relating or unifying contrasting elements. Man-made order, structure, composition, organization, form. The art of creating interesting units.

DESIGN DRAWING Any drawing made to express the true intent of a design.

DIMINUTION Objects appear smaller as their distance from the observer increases.

DRAWING The projection of an image on a surface by some instrument capable of making a mark. Drawings may be done with pencils, pens, brushes, pastels, crayons, charcoal, etching tools, and numerous other implements. Most often, drawings serve as studies or sketches for a work in some other medium, but they are frequently done as completed works in themselves.

DYNAMIC Objects or motifs in apparent motion, active, potent or energetic. (Dynamic unity is exhibited by living creatures, plants or other elements in apparent motion; such unity is flowing and active.)

ELEMENTS OF DESIGN The basic materials or factors with which all visual art is built, such as line, direction, shape, size, texture, value and colour. The visual dimensions, quantities, qualities, or attributes of units.

ELEVATION A drawing made in projection on a vertical plane, e.g. a flat drawing of the front, side or back of a house.

FORESHORTENING Equal distances appear to reduce as their distance from the observer increases. Lines of surfaces parallel to the observer's face show their maximum size. As they are revolved away from the observer they appear increasingly short.

FORM In the fine arts, form means man-made order, structure, design, composition, and organization, such as literary form, musical form, etc. Form is sometimes used as a synonym for bulk, mass, volume, and solid, connotations which are misleading and confusing if not incorrect.

GRADATION A sequence in which the adjoining parts are similar or harmonious. Transition, flowing continuity, crescendo, diminuendo, contiguous progression, regular and orderly change, blending. Steps, stairs, or scales.

GRAPHIC Concerned with drawing, painting, engraving, etching, etc.; lifelike or vividly descriptive; of diagrams or symbolic curves. Graphics is the language of design.

GRAPHIC ARTS The collective term for the pictorial arts outside painting, e.g. drawing, engraving, etching, lithography, silk-screen printing, etc. The graphic arts also include books, bookbinding, calligraphy, illustration, photography, photo-engraving, type, woodcut, etc.

GRAPHIC LITERACY The sound understanding of the principles and practices of two-dimensional representation of three-dimensional objects or views, e.g. perspective, light and shade, shadow projection, atmospheric effect, contrast, texture, colour and the elements and principles of design.

ILLUSION Perception of an object involving a false belief, deception or delusion.

ILLUSTRATION Imagery that relates explicitly to something else; that serves to clarify or adorn an anecdote, literary work, description, event, etc.

LINE A continuous, unbroken mark made by a pen, pencil, brush, or drawing instrument. Also a series of separated points or other units that lead the eye along a path.

LINEAR PERSPECTIVE The science of representing objects in three-dimensional space with line on a two-dimensional surface.

MEDIUM The vehicle or liquid with which pigment is mixed. In a more general sense, the material or method used for artistic expression (e.g. paint, metal, wood, printmaking). In technical usage the term refers to the substance used to thin or otherwise modify the pigment and its vehicle.

NEUTRAL Without distinct colouring or marks, indefinite or vague.

OBSERVER In the context of this book, the observer is the person located at the station point of a perspective construction.

ONE-LOOK PRINCIPLE The holding of the eye perfectly still at the moment of making a pictorial image of an object or view. This perfectly still eye is comparable with holding the camera lens perfectly still at the moment of pressing the shutter release.

PERSPECTIVE The common name for central projection, a scheme for representing three-dimensional objects on a two-dimensional surface in terms of relative magnitude.

PHOTOGRAPHIC REALITY The result of taking a photograph under normal lighting conditions with a 'normal' lens and producing a print without resorting to darkroom 'tricks'.

PICTORIAL REPRESENTATION The making of a rendered drawing in accordance with optical laws, i.e. perspective, light and shade, shadow, atmospheric effect etc.

PLAN A diagram or drawing created by projection on a flat surface, particularly one showing the relative position of parts of (one floor of) a building; a large-scale detailed map.

PRESENTATION DRAWING Usually a highly finished rendered perspective drawing of a design project, e.g. a building.

PRINCIPLES OF DESIGN A law of relationship or a plan of organization that determines the way in which the elements must be combined to accomplish a particular effect.

PROPORTION In the fine arts, proportion means a designated relationship of measurements. It is a ratio of intervals or of magnitudes of the same nature, kind, or class, such as time, space, length, area, angle, value or colour.

REALISM Acceptance that matter as an object of perception has real existence; truth to nature, faithful representation of perceived objects, insistence upon details.

REFLECTED LIGHT The result of direct light striking a surface and being reflected in a different direction from that surface. The angle of reflection of a light ray is equal to its angle of incidence.

RENDERING The addition to a line drawing of light and shade, shadow, values, contrast, atmospheric effect and, where required, colour to create the illusion of reality.

SCALE Relative dimensions, ratio of reduction and enlargement in a map etc. To represent in dimensions proportional to the actual ones.

SECTION A section can be described as a view of an object, e.g. a building seen when it has been cut straight through, usually in a horizontal or vertical direction.

SCIAGRAPHY The geometric construction of shadow shapes on plans, elevations and sections.

SHADE Shade exists when a surface is turned away from a light source.

SHADOW Shadow exists when an opaque object is placed between a light source and a surface on which the light would otherwise fall.

STATIC Objects without apparent motion, or forces in equilibrium. (Static unity is characteristic of a unit whose design suggests inertia, passive or formal regularity, stiffness, rigidity and uniformity.)

STATIC OR SPACE ARTS Painting, sculpture and architecture.

STATION POINT The location of the observer's eye in a perspective construction.

STYLE An individual mode of artistic expression or the characteristics of a period or subject.

TECHNICAL ILLUSTRATION A drawing or rendering done with the purpose of communicating the technical aspects of the subject rather than an artistic expression.

TECHNIQUE A mode of artistic expression or mechanical skill in the arts.

TEXTURE The quality of a surface, such as rough, smooth, matt, dull, glossy, etc. The simulation of such qualities by illusion in drawing and painting.

THREE-DIMENSIONAL SHADOW PROJECTION The method used to construct shadow shapes on a perspective projection.

TIME ARTS Music, poetry and literature.

TIME-SPACE ARTS Drama and dance.

TONE In America, tone means any value. In Britain, tone signifies the predominant value or colour of a picture and suggests its value key. (It is the British meaning that is used in this book).

TWO-DIMENSIONAL REPRESENTATION Any image of a three-dimensional object or view produced on a two-dimensional plane, such as a drawing, painting or print.

VALUE Degree of luminosity or brightness of a colour or of a neutral grey.

VANISHING POINT The point to which receding parallel lines appear to converge.

VISUAL LITERACY The understanding of the language of graphic communication.

VISUAL MESSAGES The way in which reflected light rays, or the absence of them, are combined to produce a perceived image.

Bibliography

Editions given are those consulted by the author.

Information about perspective drawing, three-dimensional shadow projection and the evolution of professional short-cut methods is contained in my books *Basic Perspective* and *Creative Perspective*.

ATKIN, W. W., R. Corbelletti, and V. R. Fiore, *Pencil Techniques in Modern Design*, New York 1953

BARBOUR, Arthur J., *Painting Buildings in Watercolour*, New York 1973

BIBIENA, Giuseppe Galli, *Architectural and Perspective Designs*, New York 1964

BISHOP, Minor L., *Architectural Renderings*, New York 1965

BOOL, F. H., Bruno Ernst, J. R. Kist, J. L. Locher and J. Wierda, *Escher, With a Complete Catalogue of the Graphic Works*, London 1982

BURDEN, Ernest, *Architectural Delineation*, New York 1971

BURKE, Joseph and Colin Caldwell, *Hogarth: The Complete Engravings*, London 1968

CALLE, Paul, *The Pencil*, New York 1971

CULLEN, Gordon, *Townscape*, New York 1966

CURTIS, Seng-gye Tombs, and Christopher Hunt, *The Airbrush Book*, London 1980

D'AMELIO, Joseph, *Perspective Drawing Handbook*, New York 1964

DESCARGUES, Pierre, *Perspective*, New York 1977

DIETERLIN, Wendel, *The Fantastic Engravings of Wendel Dieterlin, A reprint of the 1598 Edition of His Architectura*, New York 1968

DONDIS, Donis A., *A Primer of Visual Literacy*, Cambridge 1973

DORÉ, Gustave, *Perrault's Fairy Tales*, New York 1969

— *The Doré Bible Illustrations*, New York 1974

— *The Doré Illustrations for Dante's Divine Comedy*, New York 1976

— *The Doré Illustrated Balzac Droll Stories*, New York 1977

— *Doré's Illustrations for Rabelais*, New York 1978

— *Fables of La Fontaine*, London 1982

DORÉ, Gustave and Blanchard Jerrold, *London: a Pilgrimage*, New York 1970

DOYLE, Michael E., *Colour Drawing – A Marker/ Coloured Pencil Approach for Architects, Interior and Graphic Designers and Artists*, New York 1979

ERNST, Bruno, *The Magic Mirror of M. C. Escher*, New York 1976

ESCHER, M. C., *The Graphic Works of M. C. Escher*, New York 1971

ESCHER, M. C. and J. L. Locher, *The World of M. C. Escher*, New York 1971

FERRIS, Hugh, *Power in Buildings*, New York 1953

GEBHARD, David and Deborah Nevins, *200 Years of American Drawing*, New York 1977

GERDS, Donald A., *Perspective: A Step by Step Guide for Mastering Perspective by Using the Grid System*, Santa Monica, California 1980

— *Markers: Interiors, Exteriors, Product Design*, Santa Monica, California 1983

— *Markers for Advertising Comps*, Santa Monica, California 1986

GILL, Robert W., *Basic Perspective*, London and New York 1974

— *Creative Perspective*, London and New York 1975

— *The Thames and Hudson Manual of Rendering with Pen and Ink* (Revised Edition), London and New York 1984

GOSLING, Nigel, *Gustave Doré*, Newton Abbot, Devon 1973

GREGORY, R. L., *Eye and brain: the psychology of seeing*, Toronto 1969

— *The Intelligent Eye*, New York 1971

GUPTILL, Arthur L., *Rendering in Pen and Ink*, New York 1977

— *Rendering in Pencil*, New York 1977

— *Pencil Drawing Step by Step*, New York 1979

HALE, Robert Beverly and Terence Coyle, *Albinus on Anatomy*, New York 1979

HALSE, Albert O., *Architectural Rendering*, New York 1960

HELD, Richard, *Image, Object and Illusion*, San Francisco 1974

HENDERSON, Marina, *Gustave Doré: Selected Engravings*, London 1971

HOGARTH, Paul, *Drawing Architecture*, New York 1973

HULL, Joseph W., *Perspective Drawing: freehand and mechanical*, Berkeley and Los Angeles 1950

JACOBY, Helmut, *Architectural drawings*, London 1965

— *New architectural drawings*, London 1969

— *New Techniques of Architectural Rendering*, London 1971

— *Architectural Drawings 1968–76*, London 1977

JAXTHEIMER, B. W., *How to Paint and Draw*, London 1962

KAUTZKY, Theodore, *Ways with Watercolour*, New York 1963

— *Pencil Pictures*, New York 1966

— *Painting Trees and Landscapes in Watercolour*, New York 1967

— *Pencil Broadsides*, New York 1967

— *The Ted Kautzky Pencil Book*, New York 1979

KEMPER, Alfred M., *Drawings by American Architects*, New York 1973

— *Presentation Drawings by American Architects*, Somerset, N. J. 1977

KLEY, Heinrich, *The Drawings of Heinrich Kley*, New York 1962

— *More Drawings of Heinrich Kley*, New York 1962

KURTH, Dr Willy, *The Complete Woodcuts of Albrecht Dürer*, New York 1963

LAMPUGNANI, Magnago, *Visionary Architecture of the 20th Century*, London 1982

LANNERS, Edi, *Illustrations*, London 1977

LIEBERMAN, William S., *Matisse: 50 years of his graphic art*, London 1957

LOCHARD, William Kirby, *Drawing as a Means to Architecture*, New York 1968

MARTIN, C. Leslie, *Design Graphics*, New York 1962

MARTIN, Judy, *The Complete Guide to Airbrushing Techniques and Materials*, London 1983

MISSTEAR, Cecil and Helen Scott-Harman, *The Advanced Airbrush Book*, London 1984

MUGNAINI, Joseph, *Hidden Elements of Drawing*, New York 1974

OLES, Paul Stevenson, *Architectural Illustration*, New York 1979

— *Drawing the Future*, New York 1988

PAL, Imre, *Descriptive Geometry with 3-D Figures*,
Budapest 1966

PIKE, John, *John Pike Paints Watercolours*, New York
1978

PILE, John, *Drawing Architectural Interiors*, New York
1967

PIRANESI, Giovanni Battista, *The Prisons*, New York 1973

PIRANESI, Giovanni Battista and Herschel Levit, *View of
Rome Then and Now*, New York 1976

PITZ, Henry C., *Ink Drawing Techniques*, New York 1957

RAYNES, John, *Human Anatomy for the Artist*, London
1979

REEKIE, R. Fraser, *Draughtsmanship*, London 1971

— *Design in the Built Environment*, London 1972

RINES, Frank M., *Landscape Drawing*, New York 1964

RUZICKA, Jeannie, *Gustave Doré: Illustrations to Don
Quixote*, London 1974

SAUNDERS, J. B. de C. M. and Charles D. O'Malley (eds),
*The Illustrations from the Works of Andreas Vesalius of
Brussels*, New York 1950

SCHLEMM, Betty L., *Painting with Light*, New York 1978

SCHMALTZ, Carl, *Watercolour Your Way*, New York 1978

STAMPFLE, Felice, *Giovanni Battista Piranesi: Drawings in
the Piermont Morgan Library*, New York 1978

STANTON, Reggie, *Drawing and Painting Buildings: Reggie
Stanton's Guide to Architectural Rendering*, New York
1978

STRAUSS, Walter L. (ed.), *The Complete Engravings,
Etchings & Drypoints of Albrecht Durer*, New York
1973

SZABO, Marc, *Drawing File*, New York 1976

SZABO, Zoltan, *Painting Nature's Hidden Treasures*, New
York 1982

VRIES, Jan Vredeman de, *Perspective*, New York 1968

WANG, Thomas C., *Pencil Sketching*, New York 1977

WATSON, Ernest W., *The Art of Pencil Drawing*, New
York 1968

— *Courses in Pencil Sketching: Four Books in One*, New
York 1978

WATSON, Ernest W. and Aldren Watson, *The Watson
Drawing Book*, New York 1962

WERNER, Alfred, *Drawings of Albrecht Durer*, New York
1970

WILLIAMS, Raymond (ed.), *Contact: Human Communication and its History,* London and New York 1981

WORTH, Leslie, *The Practice of Watercolour Painting,* London 1977

ZIGROSSER, Carl, *Prints and Drawings of Käthe Kollwitz,* New York 1969

Acknowledgments

To the following people the author wishes to express his special appreciation for their highly valued aid in writing this book.

To Beryl M. Gill for her advice about the material and untiring efforts in checking the text.

To Michael Hope of the Melbourne School of Photography for the photographs used in this book.

To Paul Stevenson Oles and the late Davis Bité for permission to use their drawings.

List of Illustrations

Measurements are given in inches then centimetres, height before width

25 FRANCESCO GUARDI
Piazza di S. Marco,
Venice, *c.* 1777–8
Pen and wash over black
chalk
10 x 6¹/₂ (25.5 x 16.6)
British Museum,
London

30 The Surface of the Moon
Photographed from
Apollo II Lunar Module
Copyright NASA

53 GIUSEPPE GALLI
BIBIENA
Stage Design for a
Prison, 18th Century
Watercolour
Graphische Sammlung
Albertina, Vienna

68 GIAMBATTISTA PIRANESI
Engraving from the
Carceri d'Invenzione,
1750, plate III, 1st state
British Museum,
London

72 ALBRECHT DÜRER
Draughtsman Drawing a
Lute, 1525
Woodcut
51⁵/₈ x 74 (131 x 188)

81 VINCENT VAN GOGH
Vagrant with Hat and
Stick, 1882
Pencil on paper
19⁵/₈ x 12 (50 x 30.5)
Van Gogh Foundation,
Stedelijk Museum,
Amsterdam

88 Palaeolithic Cave
Painting
Bison,
15,000–10,000 BC.
Lascaux Caves, France

89 ALBRECHT DÜRER
The Four Horsemen of
the Apocalypse, 1498
Woodcut
15¹/₂ x 11¹/₈ (39.3 x 28.3)
British Museum,
London

100 HANS HOLBEIN the
Younger
Georg Gisze, 1532
Tempera on oak
37⁷/₈ x 33³/₄ (96.3 x 85.7)
Gemäldegalerie,
Staatliche Museen,
Berlin

132 CANALETTO
Venice: The Libreria and
Doge's Palace; in front
of them the Bucintoro,
1729
Pen and ink
8¹/₄ x 12¹/₂ (21.1 x 31.7)
Royal Library, Windsor
Reproduced by gracious
permission of Her
Majesty the Queen

139 GIAMBATTISTA PIRANESI
Foundations of the
Castel S. Angelo
Etching from the
Antichità Romane,
1756, volume IV, plate
IX

174 REMBRANDT
The Omval, 1645
Etching and drypoint
7¹/₄ x 8⁷/₈ (18.5 x 22.5)
British Museum,
London

176 CANALETTO
Arch with a Lantern,
c. 1744
Etching
11⁵/₈ x 16⁵/₈ (29.7 x 42.3)

192 LEONARDO DA VINCI
Bust of a Warrior,
c. 1478
Silver point
11¹/₈ x 8¹/₈ (28.5 x 20.7)
British Museum,
London

193 ALBRECHT DÜRER
Portrait of his Mother,
1514
Charcoal
16³/₄ x 11⁷/₈ (42.1 x 30.3)
Kupferstichkabinett,
Staatliche Museen,
Berlin

194 RAPHAEL
Study for the Figure of
Poetry, 1509
Grey chalk over sketch
squared in black chalk
14¹/₈ x 8⁵/₈ (36 x 22)
Royal Library, Windsor
Reproduced by gracious
permission of Her
Majesty The Queen

195 REMBRANDT
A Woman Asleep,
c. 1655–6
Brush and bistre, wash
9⁵/₈ x 8 (24.5 x 20.3)
British Museum,
London

196 EDGAR DEGAS
The Bath, 1885
Pastel
26 x 20³/₄ (66 x 52.7)
Norton Simon
Foundation, Pasadena,
California

197 PAUL CÉZANNE
Dr Gachet's House,
1873
Oil on canvas
18¹/₈ x 15 (46 x 38)
Musée d'Orsay, Paris

198 AMEDEO MODIGLIANI
Jeanne Hébuterne,
c. 1919
13¹/₂ x 11 (34.2 x 28)
Kupferstichkabinett,
Basle

199 EGON SCHIELE
Albert Paris von
Gütersloh, 1919
Lithograph
10¹/₈ x 11³/₄ (25.6 x 30)
Photo Fischer Fine Art
Ltd, London

200 KÄTHE KOLLWITZ
Self-Portrait, 1934
Lithograph
8¹/₈ x 7³/₈ (20.8 x 18.7)
Kupferstichkabinett,
Staatliche Museen,
Berlin

Index